# 1001

## WAYS
## TO CUT
## YOUR
## EXPENSES

## Also by Jonathan D. Pond

*Safe Money in Tough Times*

*Pond's Personalized Financial Planning Guide for Teachers and Employees of Educational Institutions*

*Pond's Personalized Financial Planning Guide for Salespeople*

*Pond's Personalized Financial Planning Guide for Self-Employed Professionals and Small Business Owners*

*Pond's Personalized Financial Planning Guide for Doctors, Dentists, and Health-Care Professionals*

# 1001

## WAYS TO CUT YOUR EXPENSES

JONATHAN D. POND

A DELL TRADE PAPERBACK

A DELL TRADE PAPERBACK

Published by
Dell Publishing
a division of
Bantam Doubleday Dell Publishing Group, Inc.
666 Fifth Avenue
New York, New York 10103

ISBN: 0-440-50495-3

Printed in the United States of America

# ACKNOWLEDGMENTS

The best role models of frugal living are our senior citizens, particularly those who lived through the Depression, when everyone had to cut back. They know how to get the most out of their money, and they justifiably look with horror on the spending habits of the "younger generation." Three cheap people I've known and loved deserve special recognition: two Madeleines and one mother-in-law. The first Madeleine is my mother, a good Connecticut Yankee who to this day requests a table by the window in restaurants because, she was taught, if you sit by the window, the restaurant will give you larger portions so that passersby will be enticed into patronizing the establishment. The second Madeleine, another marvelous septuagenarian, has always managed quite well, thank you, without air conditioning in her car. It's not that she can't afford it, it's because she "doesn't need it." If only all of us were so adept at distinguishing between "needs" and "wants." My mother-in-law has also been influential: She can stretch a dollar like no one else. All three have been inspirational—cheap, but inspirational.

Several very capable people have assisted in the preparation of this book, including Don Carleton, Viveca Gardiner, Natalie Liu, Jim Lowell, and Elizabeth Randolph. Jeanne Cavelos, my editor at Dell, has been very helpful, as always. Now it's my turn to help you, Jeanne: Quit the TV shopping!

Finally and foremost, I thank my long-suffering family. It's bad enough having an author as a husband and father, but it's worse when the author comes home every night with twenty new ideas about how the family can cut back on its expenses.

# ACKNOWLEDGMENTS

# CONTENTS

# ♦ III ♦

## SHOPPING

# ♦ IV ♦

## BIG-TICKET ITEMS

# ♦ V ♦

## RELATIONSHIPS

# • VI •

## FAMILY FINANCES

# • VII •

## YOUR CAREER

# • VIII •

## LEISURE

# ◆IX◆

## LATER LIFE

# ◆X◆

## PUTTING SAVINGS INTO ACTION

# Introduction

This is a book about living *beneath* your means—about spending less than you earn. Everywhere you turn, someone is trying to entice you into spending more money. It's about time we learned how to spend *less* money. Cutting down on expenses is something many of us are unaccustomed to. It seems so foreign—so un-American—so painful. But it isn't, really. You can put your expenses on a diet without suffering hunger pangs. This book will show you how. You will see how ridiculous many of our spending habits are. You will see why conspicuous consumption is no longer envied as it was in the go-go 1980s; it's now more likely to be ridiculed.

Frugality is in, and this book shows you 1001 ways to join the "in crowd." From the first tip ("Be happy with what you've got") to the 1001st tip ("Ask to be cremated"), you will find numerous money-saving ideas that you can put into practice today and forever. Getting your expenses under control so that you can save the money that is so necessary to your financial peace of mind is now within your grasp. You'll like the feeling, because when you spend less than you earn, you'll:

- *No longer* have to live paycheck to paycheck—wondering how you'll be able to meet next month's bills.
- *No longer* have to be concerned about losing everything if you lose your job.
- *No longer* feel compelled to keep up with your friends and neighbors. Let them spend themselves into financial chaos if they want to.

- *No longer* have to worry about whether you'll be able to afford to retire, or, if you're retired already, worry that you'll run out of money.

Whether you want to start saving a few dollars a week or you must save hundreds of dollars a week, you'll find that it is possible to cut your expenses to meet life's financial challenges. There's no better time to start than now.

# I

# GETTING STARTED

1

GETTING
STARTED

# 1

# Living Beneath Your Means— Without Suffering

Let's get down to business—the business of spending less money. Follow along for just a minute, and you'll see how essential it is to get into the habit of spending less and saving more.

First, for virtually everyone, *financial security* means being able to meet life's big expenses, which often include:

- Buying a home
- Educating the children
- Meeting the adversities that life may deal us, such as unemployment and disability, and
- Most important, being able to retire comfortably without ever having to worry about running out of money

Second, we cannot rely on others to provide sufficient resources to achieve financial security. We must accumulate some *investments* on our own.

Third, the only sure way to get money to *invest* is to *save regularly*.

Fourth, the only way to save regularly is to *spend less than you earn*.

Fifth, there is no secret to spending less than you earn—it's just a matter of *living beneath your means*.

Let me be more blunt: *People who don't get into the habit of living beneath their means—saving regularly—will never achieve financial security*.

Financial security is not so much dependent on how much you *earn* as it is on how much you *spend*. Many rich people spend more than they earn; many people of very modest means spend a lot less than they earn. There are people out there who have the same income as you, the same number of mouths to feed, and the same rent or mortgage to pay, but they are probably spending a lot less than you are.

## Why Is It So Difficult to Cut Down on Our Spending?

We all know how important it is to spend less so that we can save more, but far too few of us do a good job at it. Statistics show Americans to be abysmal savers. Our society worships the good life. We can't let our neighbors, friends, or coworkers beat us in the game of acquiring "things." Advertisers tell us how important it is to have "things"; if we don't have them, we are made to feel that we have failed. To give you an idea of how acquisitive we have become, many bankruptcy attorneys are reporting the absolute unwillingness of near-bankrupt people to take action to avert bankruptcy—to give up their second homes, their boats, their late-model cars, and other trappings of the wealth they don't possess. As precarious as their financial situation is, they feel *entitled* to them. This is how bad it has become.

## Room for Improvement

Even the people who have good savings habits may need to do better if they are going to achieve financial security. Retiring comfortably is becoming more difficult with each passing year because of a variety of trends, including longer life expectancies, higher inflation, earlier retirement, and a shift in the burden of funding retirement income needs away from the employer to the employee. These trends make it all the more important to cut down on spending—and the sooner the better.

## How to Develop Your Own Cost-Cutting Plan

Once you set your mind to it, cutting expenses is really quite easy. This book is chock-full of cost-cutting ideas. Some are downright practical and sensible; others are fun, and even outrageous. Most will save you money right off the bat; others take more time or require you to spend some money in order to save money. Finally, a few will save money for your heirs—a roundabout way of saying you have to die to reap the financial benefits.

Whatever your financial situation, I suggest that you do the following:

1. Take the self test in Chapter 2. It will examine your approach to spending. You will also receive a grading sheet and "teacher's comments" about your responses.

2. Set a target for how much you would like to cut your expenses. Above all, be reasonable. Don't be so ambitious at first that you have no chance at meeting your spending reduction target—you'll end up so discouraged that you'll go back to your old spend, spend, spend ways. To begin, see which category best fits you:

• *"It's impossible for me to reduce my spending."* If I had a nickel for each time someone said this to me, I would be a rich man today. If you have difficulty saving anything, *start small*. Even $5 or $10 per week is a good beginning. Show yourself that you can do it. Then, when you next get a raise, add the amount of money you net from your raise to your savings. Do this, and you're well on the way to financial stability.

• *"I've got serious financial problems. I'd be happy just to keep up with my loan payments and bills."* Millions of American families are financially endangered. Too much debt, unemployment, uninsured medical expenses, and flat or declining incomes put tremendous pressures on a family's finances. These families have no choice but to put their spending on a crash diet. This book will help you identify many cost-efficient strategies that can help you survive these financially tough times.

• *"I've saved a little over the years, but I need to do better."* You have plenty of company. You've demonstrated to yourself that you can live beneath your means, but you do so either sporadically or you just aren't saving enough. Do you know how much you should be saving? At least 10 percent of your *gross* (not net) income. Do contributions you make to your company retirement plans count? Sure they do, but you still need to save outside of your retirement plan. Ideally, you should be saving 15 to 20 percent of your income. If you are middle-aged or older and don't have money set aside for retirement, 20 percent—or more—may be necessary if you want to retire comfortably.

• *"I enjoy saving, and I do a pretty good job at it."* Even if you are one of those rare individuals who strives to pare their living expenses to the bone, you'll find even more ways to squeeze out some savings in these pages. In this day and age of avoiding extremes in anything we do, rest assured that it is almost impossible to be accused of saving too much.

Whatever your situation, indicate the amount you would like to reduce your monthly spending by:

I plan to reduce my monthly

spending by $ _____

3. Review the 1001 ways to cut your expenses. Concentrate on areas of particular interest or relevance to your own financial life. For example, my wife spends too much on clothes, so I hope she will look very carefully at the cost-cutting tips in Chapter 8, "Clothing." When you find a way that you can use, mark it. You also might want to crease the page so you can easily refer back to an important cost-cutting tip. Another suggestion is to exercise your financial muscle: Set aside fifteen minutes each day to read one section. In less than a month you'll achieve a cost-cutting savvy it takes most people a lifetime to learn.

4. Chapter 32 contains work sheets to help you evaluate your spending habits and devise plans to curb them in the future. One work sheet provides space to write down specific things you want to do to reduce expenses. You can also use that work sheet to estimate how much each cost-cutting maneuver will save you.

5. Finally, once you have developed your plan, *stick to it*. You'll soon find that you can afford a good future without giving up the good life.

## You Can Do It

You have so much to gain by cutting back on your living expenses. Living more frugally may have been passé in the 1980s, but it is definitely fashionable in the 1990s. Cars are perhaps the best indicator. In the 1980s we used to envy people who owned expensive cars. In the 1990s we are inclined to think, "What a waste of money." Learning to live beneath your means means so much. It's not very difficult, and it's crucial to your financial well-being—now, next year, ten years from now, for the rest of your life. You can do it!

# 2

# How Good a Penny-Pincher Are You?

**T**he following test will help you determine how good a penny-pincher you are. Don't cheat; no one but you will see your answers. After you have answered the ten yes-no questions, you can find out in the following text how you fared. Good luck!

*Yes*   *No*

☐   ☐   1. I buy things when they are on sale in order to save money.

☐   ☐   2. I replace my car every five years or less.

☐   ☐   3. When I see someone who carries his or her lunch to work or who uses public transportation, I'm thankful that I'm not so poor that I have to resort to such measures.

☐   ☐   4. I like to play the lottery—it's cheap fun.

☐   ☐   5. I prefer designer-label or name-brand clothes.

☐   ☐   6. I have difficulty paying off my entire credit card bill each month.

☐   ☐   7. I spend quite a bit more during the month of December than I spend during any other single month of the year.

☐ ☐ 8. If I lost my job tomorrow, I would have difficulty meeting my living expenses for six months.

☐ ☐ 9. I'd be happier if I had more money to spend.

☐ ☐ 10. It's very difficult to save money.

## Penny-Pincher Test—Grading Sheet

Grading your test:

1. Add up the number of "yes" responses.
2. Your evaluation is presented below:

| Number of "Yes" Responses | Evaluation |
| --- | --- |
| 0 to 2 | *El cheapo.* Congratulations, you make the late Jack Benny look like a big spender. Keep up the good work! |
| 3 to 5 | To spend is human, but to save is divine. You've got a good handle on your financial life, but there's still room for improvement. Go directly to the 1001 ways. |
| 6 to 8 | Danger: deficits ahead. You must have learned your spending habits from the federal government. Before it's too late, learn some good money-saving habits in these pages. |
| 9 or 10 | Step aside, Imelda. You're well on your way to becoming one of the world's big spenders. I'm surprised you could afford to buy this book. But there are ways to cut back on expenses— 1001 ways. |

Please refer to the following comments for any questions you answered "yes."

## Penny-Pincher Test—Teacher's Comments

The numbers here refer to those in the questionnaire:

1. No one in the history of the world has ever "saved" money by buying something on sale—they've *spent* money. It's fine to buy things that you genuinely need when they're on sale, but all too often we just think we need something when it's on sale.

2. Cars are the world's second biggest waste of money. (See number 4 below for the world champion.) Unless you buy an old car in the first place (a great idea), you should trade cars no more frequently than every seven to ten years.

3. People who use public transportation (or who carpool) and who brown-bag it at work are probably saving a couple of thousand dollars a year compared with those who drive in to work and buy their lunch. Don't pity them, emulate them.

4. Lotteries are nothing more than a tax on the naive. A dollar or two a week *is* cheap fun, but most lottery players spend far more, and they are simply throwing hard-earned money away.

5. It's so easy to justify our spending habits. When it comes to clothing, the Madison Avenue advertising agencies help us feel good about overspending on "up-to-date" designer fashions (translation: They'll be out-of-date in six months) and "long-lasting" brand-name clothing (translation: If you buy enough of these high-priced clothes, the advertising agency will have a long-lasting relationship with the manufacturer).

6. There is one reason why you may not want to pay off your entire credit card balance—if you just love to pay 19.8 percent interest on the unpaid balance.

7. You really know when you've got your spending under control if you can spend at the same rate between Thanksgiving and New Year's that you spend between New Year's and Thanksgiving.

8. Imagine how much better you'd sleep at night if you knew that, should you lose your job (or become disabled), you could get by financially for many months. Spending brings momentary satisfaction; saving brings lasting peace of mind.

9. Most people think they'd be on Easy Street if only they earned another $10,000. Nonsense. If you're not happy with

what you've now got, you won't be happier if you had more to spend.

10. Everyone can save money, and everyone can save more money than they're now saving. It is inexcusable not to be saving at least 10 percent of your *gross* income, although 15 to 20 percent is better. (It's impossible to "oversave.") On the other hand, if you haven't been able to save much, if anything, start small—even $5 or $10 per week. You'll like the feeling of living beneath your means, so you'll eventually want to save more. Then you'll be hooked. Saving is a marvelous addiction.

## THE HALL OF SHAME:
### The Twenty-Five Biggest Wastes of Your Money

Now that you know where you stand as a penny-pincher, look at this list of shame and see if you've fallen victim to any of these money wasters:

1. Lotteries
2. Buying a new car every few years
3. Anything that's "new and improved"
4. Credit life insurance
5. Investing on the advice of someone you've never met
6. Fancy restaurants
7. Buying something on sale that you don't need
8. Courses that teach you how to buy real estate for no money down
9. Optional cable television services
10. Investing in something you don't understand
11. Life insurance for children
12. Spending vested pension benefits when you change jobs rather than rolling them over into an IRA
13. Boats
14. Credit card loans
15. Buying property you've never seen
16. Gold cards
17. Lavishing expensive gifts on loved ones and friends— or on yourself
18. Driving to work alone
19. Lending money to friends
20. Holding on to investments for sentimental reasons

21. Sunroofs
22. Designer-label clothing
23. Low-interest savings accounts
24. Buying anything to keep up with the Joneses, such as family beepers or sit-down lawnmowers
25. TV shopping

Okay, so almost all of us have room for improvement. That's what this book is all about. Check out these 1001 ways designed to help you live beneath your means, and see how many you can incorporate into your life.

# II

# YOUR HOME

# 3

# Housekeeping

**D**etergent, paper towels, trash bags, small appliances. Housekeeping expenses seem to be minor compared with many of the "big-ticket items" we have to buy from time to time. But if you're not careful, these seemingly small expenses add up to big money. The reason? There's no end to housekeeping. As soon as we take care of one chore, another needs doing, and the chore we completed last week needs to be done again next week.

The following tips will help you keep your housekeeping expenses under control. We'll tour your home, and you'll find a lot of small moneysaving ideas that can help take the pinch out of the hidden expenses of maintaining your abode.

## ◆ 1  Be happy with what you've got.

First things first. Most of us spend more than we should because we try to maintain a life-style beyond our means. The only way you'll be able to achieve financial peace of mind and, ultimately, financial security is to live *beneath* your means, and the only way to live beneath your means comfortably is to be happy with what you've already got. If you spend some time thinking about all you have rather than all you'd like to have, you'll probably discover that you're already quite fortunate.

## ◆ 2  Read the label.

Always follow storage and care instructions on clothing and food. Spoilage and discards are money down the drain.

### ◆ 3   Buy it to last.

Many people seem to have forgotten that nondisposable razors and cloth napkins still exist. These items will cost you more than their short-lived counterparts in the short term, but they'll save you money in the long run.

### ◆ 4   Organize your storage rather than pay rent to a miniwarehouse.

Miniwarehouses were a great growth industry in the 1980s. I guess we were acquiring so much so quickly during the "decade of greed" that we couldn't store it all in our own homes. Having a miniwarehouse was probably a status symbol. As you were pulling out of your driveway you could say to your neighbor, "I'm off to the miniwarehouse to pick up our Wedgwood service for sixty for tonight's banquet." In the 1990s, this kind of nonsense is out. A little organization of your in-house storage area will almost certainly allow room for everything you have acquired. If you still have too much after you have reorganized your storage, hold a yard sale.

### ◆ 5   Be prepared to make emergency repairs.

The only thing that can be said with certainty about household emergencies is that they are certain to happen. Whenever one happens, you need to know quickly how to keep matters from getting worse. Whether it is a power failure, a clogged drain, a leaky roof, or any other household disorder, be prepared for the inevitable so that when it occurs you can handle the disruption.

### ◆ 6   Always try to do it yourself before getting someone else to do it.

Unless the task is dangerous, this advice holds true for, among other things, minor home repairs, renovations, cleaning, plumbing, car maintenance, tax preparation, and laundry.

## ♦ 7 Get into the "recycle" habit.

Return cans/metals/plastic bags for money. You can get paid to recycle some items, such as cans. Recycle also means use again. Be creative about reusing objects.

## ♦ 8 Don't automatically assume that a broken appliance must be replaced.

Typical response to discovering that an appliance is pooping out: "Yippee! I can go out and buy a new one, and this time it will have all sorts of new and improved features." Hold on a minute. Don't use a broken appliance as an excuse to go out and spend more money than you need to. First, find out what's wrong with it. You may be pleasantly surprised that the TV or dishwasher or stereo can be fixed at little cost. And don't get depressed that you won't be able to "upgrade." As an old New England saying goes, "Use it up, wear it out, make it do, or do without."

## ♦ 9 Save receipts for major purchases.

If you ever have a problem with an item you purchased, you're going to need the receipt. Set up a file for important receipts. The best place to store them is away from your premises—in your office, perhaps, so if disaster strikes, you'll be able to show the insurance company what you owned and how much you paid for your expensive possessions.

## ♦ 10 Put all warranties and owner's manuals in one location.

Although most products you buy that have a warranty will not break down until the week after the warranty expires, you should still put the warranties and the owner's manuals in a single location so you can find them if needed. Also, the owner's manual can help you troubleshoot when a problem pops up and may help you avoid an unnecessary trip to the "nearest" service center (usually a three-day drive away).

## ◆ 11 Do small home remodeling projects yourself.

Do you go to the Yellow Pages when you need to make some small improvements to your living quarters? Don't automatically call someone in. Even if you can't distinguish a hammer from a screwdriver, you may well be able to do it yourself. First go to a bookstore (or, better, a library, so you don't have to pay for the book) to check out one of the many excellent references on home improvements. After reading about your "project" you can probably get some advice from the local hardware or home supply store. Sure it may take some time and effort, but imagine the money you'll be saving—not to mention the pride in having done it yourself.

## ◆ 12 Inventory your household possessions.

This is something to do on a rainy Saturday, because it's boring, but a good household inventory can save you a lot of money in the event disaster strikes. Imagine this: You come home from work one day to witness the fire department bulldozing the last charred remains of your dwelling into what used to be the cellar. Would you be able to provide your insurance company with a detailed list of what you owned? Probably not. By taking a detailed inventory, best done with a handwritten list accompanied by photographs of your possessions, you can rest assured that if disaster strikes you will be well situated to get a fair settlement from your insurance company. By the way, don't store your inventory in the house. Better to put the list and photographs in your safe deposit box or in your desk drawer at work.

## ◆ 13 Develop a family fire-escape plan.

A family fire-escape plan could save your life or the life of a family member. Don't risk the cost in both human and financial terms of injury, death, and/or loss of personal property caused by a too-time-consuming escape from a house or apartment fire.

### ◆ 14    Use sponges more and paper towels less.

How can they make paper towel rolls that last less than a day so thick? Resist the Pavlovian response to go to the paper towel roll. Instead, reach for the sponge.

### ◆ 15    Use grocery bags as trash can liners.

We are an overly "trash-bagged" society. Most families have carton upon carton of variously sized trash bags. Some are scented, some are three-ply (it sounds like a steel-belted radial tire); all are expensive. On the other hand, we bring home grocery bag after grocery bag, only to throw them into our designer trash bags. Grocery bags, whether paper or plastic, make perfectly satisfactory trash can liners.

### ◆ 16    Reuse plastic trash bags.

Once they fill up a trash bag, most people figure that that bag's life is over. We're so wasteful. Many times, however, the trash bag is simply filled with papers or other innocuous items. Why not empty the trash bag out into a trash can or a larger trash bag and reuse it?

### ◆ 17    Reuse plastic containers.

Don't throw out those plastic food containers. They have a variety of uses, particularly when you want to store something, whether it's food or crayons, paper clips or buttons.

### ◆ 18    Use "old-fashioned" multipurpose household products (e.g., ammonia, boric acid, baking soda) rather than heavily marketed single-purpose products.

Use ammonia, water, dishwasher soap, or liquid detergent to remove stains. Use baking soda instead of toothpaste. Use alcohol wipes and baking soda or talcum instead of deodorant.

## ◆ 19 Make your own cleaning fluids rather than buying them.

There are a lot of cleaning fluids you can make out of commonly available materials—vinegar and lemon juice, for example. Several books are available to help you put together your own homemade compounds, and you'll swear they do a better job than the store-bought brands.

## ◆ 20 Wash your windows on the cheap.

Add one-half cup of ammonia or white vinegar to one gallon of water. Use this home-brew window washing fluid along with crumpled sheets of newspaper to wash and dry your windows.

## ◆ 21 Organize your kitchen utensils.

Recently I went into one of our kitchen drawers to fetch a corkscrew. It didn't take too long to find one: There were seven corkscrews in the drawer. The sad fact is that over the years our kitchen utensils were so poorly organized that we could never find anything. The only solution is to buy another "one." Well, we reorganized our kitchen and suggest you do the same.

## ◆ 22 Use a knife sharpener to refurbish old knives.

Change your inclination to throw something out long before it is no longer useful. For example, when properly sharpened, a good knife will give you many years of devoted service. If your knife is not serving you, sharpen it. You don't necessarily need to buy a knife sharpener; a whetstone will restore the blade.

## ◆ 23 Try using your dishwasher with less detergent.

Are you scared to death to use less than the manufacturer recommends? While your fears are well founded with such things as oil in your car, there are many things you can probably use less of. Dishwasher detergent is one. The worst that could happen when you experiment with less detergent is that you'll have to run the dishes again, but chances are you'll do just as well with less.

### ♦ 24  Save packing materials.

There is no reason to buy a box or bubble wrap to prepare a package for mailing. When you receive something in the mail or buy something that comes in a sturdy carton, save it. Also, save any packing material, including those awful Styrofoam "peanuts" that scatter all over the floor. You're accomplishing two things by saving packing materials: First, recycling, and the environment will thank you. Second, you'll always have packing materials on hand, so you'll avoid hopping into your car to go buy some overpriced packing material.

### ♦ 25  Go through drawers for paper clips, pens, and pencils.

If you go through your kitchen, dresser, and desk drawers in search of stray paper clips, pens, and pencils, I can promise you that you will find enough of these items to last your lifetime.

### ♦ 26  Clean your house yourself.

Sure, it's convenient having someone clean your house, but it's also a big expense. If you're looking for ways to decrease your living expenses, think about cleaning your house or your apartment yourself. If this is too much for you to endure, consider reducing the frequency with which you now have your house cleaned.

### ♦ 27  Reuse vacuum cleaner bags.

Don't throw out vacuum cleaner bags. You can get two or three bagsful out of a single vacuum cleaner bag. The savings are small, but they're savings nonetheless.

### ♦ 28  Wash your shower curtain.

One way to avoid getting mildew on your shower curtains is never to use the shower. If you're unwilling to do that, you

still may be able to get rid of the mildew without replacing
the curtain. Throw it into the washing machine with a couple
of towels, and be pleased with the result.

### ◆ 29  Use duct tape to repair torn ring holes in a shower curtain.

Is duct tape the greatest household item ever invented? Probably. It can perform a lot of tough jobs, including repairing
the ring holes in the shower curtain, which always tear long
before the shower curtain is ready for retirement.

### ◆ 30  Sew a worn-out contour sheet to a flat mattress pad to make a fitted mattress pad.

Cheap, cheap, cheap. So what? No one will know the difference anyway. Go out and price fitted versus flat mattress
pads, and you won't think this is such a silly idea.

### ◆ 31  Cut unwearable panty hose into strips and use them as string.

If you want a couple of miles of panty hose string, contact my
mother-in-law. It works well and it's particularly useful for
tying garden plants.

### ◆ 32  Make braided rugs, pot holders, etc., from old nylon stockings.

A little dye and a little ingenuity can turn old nylon hosiery
into a durable rug or pot holder.

### ◆ 33  Make pillowcases from old sheets.

The sides of old sheets probably don't have much wear, so
turn them into pillowcases.

### ◆ 34  Make dishtowels from old linen or cotton tablecloths.

Take the scissors to an old tablecloth and turn it into a top-
of-the-line dishtowel.

## ◆ 35　Make aprons from old cotton house-dresses.

You'll never have to buy an apron again if you just recycle a cotton housedress that would otherwise be thrown out.

## ◆ 36　Don't install carpets in high-traffic areas.

If you're blessed with usable wood floors, consider keeping the floors bare in high-traffic areas. Although the science of carpet making has come a long way, high-traffic areas will do the carpet in long before other areas show any signs of wear.

## ◆ 37　Use discarded carpeting to line shelves.

If you're replacing carpet, try cutting up the old carpet, washing it, and lining your shelves with it. What's nice about carpet shelf liner is that it's washable and therefore will last nearly forever.

## ◆ 38　Install a home security system yourself.

This can cut costs considerably. Examine the various types of do-it-yourself systems available. You'll find one that meets your antiburglar needs.

## ◆ 39　Keep an extra set of keys handy.

If you haven't done so already, go right over to the keymaker and have a complete duplicate set of your keys made. Store them in a safe but accessible place. When next you lose your keys, you'll save a bundle in locksmith's fees.

## ◆ 40　Frame it yourself.

The three biggest expenses in your life are housing, automobiles, and picture framing. You can spend a hundred dollars framing a $10 print. Unless cost is no object (and if it is, you probably shouldn't be reading this book), there are ways to cut the cost of picture framing. One is to do it yourself. Most cities have do-it-yourself framing shops replete with people to help you. Also, you may be able to use ready-made rather than custom-made frames. This would save you money even if you had to hire a professional to do it.

### ◆ 41 Rent rather than buy items that you will only use occasionally.

Americans love to buy gadgets. All too often we buy something because we have some home project to accomplish, but once the project is complete, we don't use the chain saw or leaf blower or carpet shampooer. So think very carefully before buying. You may be better off renting it. These days you can rent just about anything.

### ◆ 42 Organize your tools.

So you won't go out and buy something you actually have but can't find.

### ◆ 43 Use old oven mittens for gardening gloves.

Well-used oven mittens are so gross that we're inclined simply to throw them out if washing them doesn't do any good. But they make marvelous gardening gloves, particularly if you're working among thorns and other such unpleasantries.

### ◆ 44 Buy a push lawn mower.

If you have the proverbial "postage stamp" yard, is there really any reason why you need a power lawn mower? A push mower is cheaper to buy and to maintain, and the additional exercise may keep the doctor bills in check.

### ◆ 45 Popsicle sticks make great plant markers.

Kids can find a thousand things to do with Popsicle sticks, and you can find at least one: Use them to identify plants or crops in your garden.

### ◆ 46 Keep a sheet of paper handy to write down household items that are needed the next time you go shopping.

If you use your last sixty-watt light bulb to replace one that burns out, chances are about ninety-nine in a hundred that you won't remember to buy more light bulbs the next time you go shopping. These things need to be written down; otherwise you'll constantly be making trips to and fro. Put a sheet of notepaper on the refrigerator door or some other obvious location and use it.

# 4

# Homeowners

**A**hhhh, the pleasures of home ownership. A place to call home—a place that you own or, more likely, you'll own after you've made another 274 mortgage payments. In the meantime, the happy homeowner has to put up with (and pay for) peeling paint, clogged sewer pipes, failed heating/air-conditioning systems, holes in the roof, basement floodings—the list seems endless. Following is a litany of suggestions that will help bring the high costs of home ownership back down to earth. Whether you already own a home, are in the market for a first home, or are contemplating a move, this chapter's for you.

## ◆ 47  Get several bids on home repair or improvement projects.

Curiously, studies have shown that homeowners rarely take the lowest bid on home repair or home improvement projects. All too often they fail to obtain several bids, although—take my own recent experience—it's profitable doing so. We needed some work on the chimney, and the first quote came in at an astonishing $3,500. The second quote came in at $3,500 as well. We almost concluded that the best we could do was a $3,500 chimney repair bill, but a third, highly recommended company did the job for $750. The problem: the other two companies were inflexible about the way they repaired chimneys, while the third company was client-oriented in its approach.

## ♦ 48 Negotiate fees or ask for competitive quotes.

After you've decided on the company or person to handle your home repairs or improvements, the quotation may still be negotiable. You may feel awkward trying to get a quotation dropped a bit, but remember, it's your money you're spending. There may be a little slack in the bid. Don't get too bold, but then again don't pass up the opportunity to save a few bucks.

## ♦ 49 Don't fall for home improvement scams.

Home improvement scams are on the rise. All homeowners are vulnerable, particularly the elderly. Always take your sweet time deciding whether to go ahead with a home improvement. Always check out the person who wants to do the work. One clear warning sign: The home improver came to you rather than you going to them. If you have elderly parents, encourage them to check with you before committing to any kind of home repair or home improvement, no matter how small.

## ♦ 50 Don't make foolish home renovations.

Just as there are good reasons to borrow and bad reasons to borrow, so there are good home renovations and bad home renovations. A good home renovation will add value to the home when you sell it. They include adding living space, adding or modernizing bathrooms, adding kitchens, etc. On the other hand, swimming pools, boccie ball courts, or a rooftop turret to house your hobby telescope won't add much, if any, value to your house. In fact, some renovations will actually detract from the value of your home.

## ♦ 51 Never own the best home in the neighborhood.

Never make improvements to your home to the point where it is the fanciest abode in the neighborhood. Also, never purchase the best home in the neighborhood. The reason is that when you sell your home, you'll discover that the priciest homes in a neighborhood don't appreciate as much as the more modest houses do. In other words, you won't get as much of a return on your home investment. 'Tis far better to own and maintain a modest home in a nice neighborhood.

### ◆ 52  Bargain hard when you purchase a home.

The problem with the process of buying a home is that we become emotionally attached to it before we have even purchased it. In particular, first-time home buyers tend to be poor negotiators. One piece of advice: Talk with relatives or friends who have purchased several houses over the years. They should be able to guide you through the process so you don't leave too much money on the table. The sooner you learn to be hard-nosed in bargaining down a house price, the better. Remember, it's just a house until you've bought it; then it will be your home.

### ◆ 53  Closing costs are negotiable.

Sure, there are traditions that usually dictate which closing costs are borne by the purchaser (most) and which by the seller (very few). But there is no law dictating who pays what. If you're a savvy purchaser, you may want to try to get the seller to agree to paying some of the costs normally paid by you, the purchaser. What have you got to lose? If you're doing a mortgage refinancing with the bank, remember that closing costs with the bank are negotiable as well. Some banks will reduce closing costs to get your business.

### ◆ 54  Insist on interest on any deposit you make toward the purchase of a home.

When you make a deposit upon, say, signing a purchase and sale agreement for a home, make sure that whoever holds the deposit is going to pay interest on it. Why let someone else have the use of your money?

### ◆ 55  Hire a home inspector to examine any house you want to purchase.

Never buy a house without having it inspected. If the seller will not let you have it inspected, walk away from the deal.

Ideally, you'll have the inspection before you make the offer. In that way you may be able to negotiate the offering price down because of problems the inspector will inevitably locate. At the minimum, put an inspection contingency in the purchase and sale agreement.

## ♦ 56 Avoid buying a house when the local housing market is overheated.

There was a time in the late 1980s in New England and California when a house would go on the market in the morning and by noon there would be five offers for it, all of which were over the asking price. It was a veritable feeding frenzy, and prospective home buyers were so desperate to get into a house that, as hindsight has so amply shown, they took leave of their senses. If you start hearing experts saying that housing prices are going to continue rising at double-digit annual percentage rates every year ad infinitum, don't buy. Chances are, as we're witnessing in many areas of the country, if you wait a couple of years you'll be able to avoid the frenzy and select among an almost unlimited number of houses at much, much lower prices.

## ♦ 57 Think long and hard before building your own home.

Rule number 1 when building your dream house: It will cost a lot more than you originally estimated. Rule number 2: It's an enormous hassle. The best way to control housing costs: Buy an existing home.

## ♦ 58 Buy a multifamily house.

If you're thinking of buying a home, whether it's your first home or a subsequent home, give some thought to buying a multifamily house—a duplex, a triple-decker, etc. The story goes like this: First, you can often buy "more house" than you could if you were looking for a single-family home because the mortgage lender takes into consideration the rent you'll be receiving. Over the years you own the multifamily house, the rent will almost certainly increase while your housing costs may stay relatively stable. Eventually you could end up garnering enough rent to cover most if not all of the cost of running the house. If you doubt me, talk to someone who has owned a two- or three-family home for a long time. They're probably sitting on a gold mine.

### ◆ 59  Move into a smaller home.

For the life of me, I can't understand why so many empty-nesters, particularly those who are retired, insist on living in the family estate when they could move into a smaller home that is more manageable to own and maintain. Even youngsters who were caught up in the housing frenzy of the 1980s may want to consider downsizing in the 1990s as part of their overall strategy to improve their finances.

### ◆ 60  Buy a home in a less expensive neighborhood.

One way to reduce housing expenses, either if you're planning to move or need to move for financial reasons, is to move into a neighborhood that is less expensive. If you've lived in a certain locale for a long time, you can probably identify wonderful neighborhoods where housing prices haven't gone through the roof. Ideally, you may find an area to live in that is in transition or that is just becoming more popular. Often these neighborhoods experience housing prices that rise most rapidly. So, with luck, moving into a less expensive neighborhood will save you money initially and will allow you to enjoy above-average appreciation of your home.

### ◆ 61  Move to a town with a lower property tax rate.

Are your property taxes going through the roof? Property tax rates often vary significantly in the same area. Even towns that border each other may have vastly different tax rates. If your property taxes are out of control, consider moving to a more hospitable town.

### ◆ 62  Move out of the city.

If you are an urban dweller, consider the suburbs. If you're a suburbanite, consider the country. Although you may have to weigh the lower housing costs against the costs of commuting, you could save quite a bit.

◆ **63**   **Resist the temptation to trade up from your current home.**

What is it with our way of life? Many of us save for years to buy a home. Yet a week after we move in we're thinking about getting a bigger house. Our parents never thought that way. They bought a house, raised the kids in it, and retired in it. Chances are you've got a pretty nice home now, so stop thinking about trading up. The only certainty about trading up is that you're going to have higher housing costs.

◆ **64**   **Move into a condominium development that has been in existence long enough to have a predictable maintenance fee.**

No one knows for sure what the cost of maintenance will be in a new condo development. I certainly wouldn't take the developer's or the broker's estimates as gospel. You may save yourself some unpleasant and expensive surprises if you buy into a condo development that has been in existence for a few years and therefore has a more predictable and stable maintenance fee.

◆ **65**   **Don't buy a vacation home.**

Let's forget the enjoyment factor of a vacation home for a moment. This isn't a book about enjoyment, anyway; it's a book on how to reduce your living expenses (without impairing your enjoyment too much). Vacation homes usually cost a ton of money to buy and maintain. And despite the breathless assertions of whomever is trying to sell you the property, renting it won't come close to covering its cost. Moreover, recessions demonstrate how vulnerable vacation home prices are to a weak economy.

◆ **66**   **Try to sell your home yourself.**

Real-estate brokers are usually essential to the successful sale of a home. However, if you've got the time, there's nothing wrong with trying to sell the home yourself. You may have to put up with some aggravation, but if you can find the right buyer, you'll save several thousand dollars in commissions. If your "for sale by owner" effort becomes too aggravating or unproductive, you can always hire a broker.

## ◆ 67 Try to bargain for more favorable terms when you take out a mortgage.

Believe it or not, mortgage terms are often negotiable. The lenders want your business, and many are willing to bend a little. Don't assume that their quoted rates and terms are inflexible. Try to knock the rate down a bit or see if they'll waive one or two "points" that you would otherwise have to pay at closing.

## ◆ 68 Condo and co-op owners should adjust the basis of their homes upward for any improvements that benefit all apartment owners.

If the condominium or cooperative makes any improvements in the building that benefit all owners, your proportionate cost of these improvements increases the tax basis of your home for purposes of computing capital gains when it is sold. Be sure to keep a record of any general improvements in addition to any improvements you make on your own.

## ◆ 69 Refinance your mortgage at a lower rate.

If mortgage interest rates drop 1½ percent or more below the current rate on your mortgage, figure out how much money you could save by refinancing. It may be worth the cost.

## ◆ 70 Improve an inefficient heating and/or air-conditioning system.

Just because your heating and/or air-conditioning system is old doesn't mean you should get rid of it. On the other hand, there probably will come a time where it makes sense for you to bite the bullet. It may take many years for savings through efficiency to pay for the new system, but it remains a worth-

while investment. Sometimes you do have to spend money to
save money.

◆ **71** **Buy a good home repair manual.**

The easiest way to turn yourself from a klutz into a quasi-
competent home repairer is to buy one of the many good
books on home repair. Armed with a good home repair book
and a positive attitude, you can save a lot of money by doing
small and perhaps medium home repairs yourself.

◆ **72** **Check the foundation of your house annually.**

Don't let an easily correctible problem turn into a financial
problem. Check for cracks, bulges, or the presence of moisture
in the basement. An ounce of prevention . . .

◆ **73** **Trim overgrown trees and shrubs.**

Don't let trees and shrubs engulf your home. Trim them back
so they don't damage siding, clog gutters, or harbor pests.

◆ **74** **Do the painting yourself.**

Certainly you have the time, if not the inclination, to do some
of the painting yourself. Perhaps you don't want to do the
exterior, but how about painting a few rooms? There are all
sorts of gadgets at your friendly paint supplier that can help
you do the job. There is also a lot of job satisfaction in
freshening up a dank room with a new coat of paint.

◆ **75** **Don't repaint an entire room if a little
touch-up will do.**

It's amazing what a little touch-up painting can do. Walls
that look like they have chicken pox transform into almost
perfect condition. If your touch-up job doesn't meet your
standards, you can still have the room repainted, but if it
does, you've saved a bit of money.

### ◆ 76    Clean out your gutters.

If you clean out your gutters annually (or pay someone to do it if you don't want to risk a ladder accident), you'll be preventing some big problems later that are caused when your gutters don't drain properly.

### ◆ 77    Have your sewer pipes cleaned every year.

An ounce of prevention will prevent pounds of sewage from backing up in your house. Clogged sewers are like clogged arteries: You often don't know there's a problem until it's too late. Spend some money each year and have your sewer pipes cleaned.

### ◆ 78    Install dead-bolt locks in your home.

The first lines of defense against intruders are good locks. They will not only give you more peace of mind, but you also may be able to get a reduction in your homeowner's insurance. Also, if they prevent a burglary, they save you money as well. (No one ever comes out even when they're burglarized.)

### ◆ 79    Appeal your property tax assessment.

Surprisingly, a large percentage of people who appeal their property tax assessments end up with a lower bill. Don't forget, property values have dropped in many areas of the country and will drop in many more as the recession continues.

### ◆ 80    Recycle to lower your trash collection fees.

If your town doesn't yet have a recycling program, it probably will someday soon. The more that townspeople recycle, the lower the trash collection fees. In fact, many towns are assessing a higher trash collection fee for homeowners who don't recycle.

### ◆ 81    Take in a boarder.

One way to cut your housing cost is to take in a boarder. People pay a lot for rent these days, and as a homeowner you may be able to offer a superior living environment to a prospective tenant. Sure, it may be inconvenient; on the other hand, you may be able to find an ideal boarder—someone who travels a lot or a quiet student.

### ♦ 82 Take advantage of the $125,000 exclusion available to home sellers over age fifty-five.

The over-55 capital gains exclusion for homesellers provides a wonderful opportunity to save a substantial amount of capital gains taxes. While the decision as to when to take the exclusion requires some evaluation for those who expect to buy and sell more than one principal residence after age fifty-five, the exclusion provides a real opportunity for older people to feather their retirement nests.

### ♦ 83 If you are going to sell your house and trade up, plan carefully to avoid incurring a capital gains tax.

The rules for postponing the profit from the sale of a home when you are replacing the previous home with a more expensive home are pretty straightforward but inflexible. Therefore you must plan very carefully so you will avoid a nasty and unnecessary capital gains tax.

### ♦ 84 If you are going to sell your residence for a loss, consider renting it for a while so you can take a tax loss when you eventually sell.

The rules get a bit tricky here, but you may be able to take a partial capital loss for tax purposes on the sale of your home in a declining real estate market if you rent it prior to its sale, thereby turning a personal residence into investment property. If you plan to do this, check it out with a tax professional.

## ◆ 85 If you rent out a vacation home, careful planning can maximize tax deductions.

Like many tax-saving techniques, careful adherence to the vacation home rules can reduce your tax bill. If you rent out your vacation home for less than fifteen days during the year, you do not have to declare any of the income you receive. If it is rented for more than fifteen days, there are still opportunities for tax advantages, but the rules get more complicated, and hence you must plan carefully.

## ◆ 86 Installment sales can postpone the payment of some capital gains tax.

If you expect to sell your home or some investment property for a large capital gain, you can use the installment sales method to spread out over several years the taxes that must be paid on the profit. Check out the details, and be sure to arrange any installment sale only with a creditworthy borrower because, in effect, you are the lender.

## ◆ 87 If you move, you may be able to deduct certain costs associated with disposing of your old residence, including closing costs if you owned a home, or, if you rented your dwelling, the costs of settling an unexpired lease.

Many costs associated with selling your house, or if you have to, paying a penalty to get out of your lease, are deductible if your move qualifies for tax deductibility.

## ◆ 88 If you are nearing age fifty-five, postponing the sale of your home could be very profitable.

If you are near age fifty-five and contemplating the sale of your home at a substantial capital gain, waiting until you qualify for the $125,000 exclusion may make sense. It's up to you, but you should consider the ramifications of moving now or delaying your move until you qualify for the over fifty-five tax break.

### ◆ 89 Keep good records of home improvements.

Accurate home improvement records may not save you money for many years, but save money they will. Home improvements, as opposed to repairs, can be added to the cost of your home to calculate capital gains. So hold on to every home improvement record to prove the adjusted cost of your home when capital gains taxes are assessed.

### ◆ 90 If you are over fifty-five and the profit from the sale of your home is over $125,000, you may still be able to avoid paying a capital gains tax on the excess profit.

By combining both the over-fifty-five exclusion and the capital-gains deferral provisions of the tax laws, you can have your cake and eat it too. First, you can take advantage of the $125,000 exclusion, and then you can postpone paying taxes on any remaining capital gains by investing in a new home whose cost is greater than the sale price of the old house minus the $125,000 exclusion.

### ◆ 91 Don't celebrate your fifty-fifth birthday by signing a purchase-and-sale agreement to take advantage of the $125,000 exclusion.

To qualify for the $125,000 exclusion the sale date of your home must be after the date on which your fifty-fifth birthday falls, not just after the start of the year in which you reach age fifty-five. So don't jump the gun.

### ◆ 92 Rental of your home may not disqualify you from the over-fifty-five $125,000 exclusion.

The general qualification rule requires that you occupy the house for at least three of the five years preceding the date of sale. Therefore, you could rent the house for two of those years—even the two years between the time you move out and the date on which the sale takes place. This could be particularly advantageous if you expect the house to appreciate considerably over the next couple of years and you don't mind renting the home before selling it.

◆ **93    Defer repairs on your home until a time when they can be included as part of a comprehensive home-improvement project.**

How can a repair be considered a home improvement? Say you want to paint your kitchen ceiling but also plan to modernize the whole room eventually. If you defer the painting until you are ready to undertake the modernization project, the cost of painting the ceiling can be included as a home improvement.

◆ **94    All is not lost if you sell your home at a loss if part of the home has been used for business or rental.**

If you sell your home at a loss, you may be able to deduct some of the loss if you maintained an office at home or a rental unit in your residence. Otherwise, none of the costs would be deductible.

◆ **95    Don't take the office-at-home deduction if you plan to take advantage of the over-fifty-five capital gains exclusion on the sale of your home.**

If you have used your home for business purposes and plan to take the over-fifty-five capital gains exclusion, you should disqualify yourself for the office-at-home deduction at least three years before the sale date. The office-at-home rules are so rigid, it's pretty easy to alter the room's use so as to disqualify yourself from the deduction and thereby be able to take advantage of the full $125,000 capital-gains tax break.

◆ **96    Try to incur presale "fixing up" expenses within ninety days of contracting to sell your home.**

The ninety-day rules for "fixing up" expenses allow you to adjust the basis of your home for capital-gains tax calculation purposes within ninety days of the execution of the contract to sell your home. While it's tough to time these things, particularly in slow real-estate markets, keep the real-estate market in mind when you're planning these cosmetic improvements to your home. For example, if you put the house on the market during a slow season, you may want to defer doing the improvements before the peak home selling season in your community.

## ◆ 97 Get a goat.

Check with the zoning authorities first. But if you get a goat, it will not only mow your lawn but will also give you milk and cheese. Such a deal.

# 5

# Renters

Housing costs are the single greatest item of expense in our budgets. If you rent, there are several things you can do to assure that you can live in an attractive apartment at a reasonable cost. The following moneysaving suggestions take you from the time you begin your search for an apartment through the end of your lease.

P.S.: If your children are renters, suggest some of these helpful ideas to them.

## ◆ 98    Negotiate your rent.

Everything in your financial life is negotiable. Don't automatically accept the initial rent offer that a landlord or broker quotes. Try for a lower rent: You have nothing to lose and a lot to gain. In many areas of the country there's so much available rental space that rents are extremely negotiable. Whether you're a new tenant or are going through a lease renewal, negotiate your rent payments.

## ◆ 99    Avoid buildings that lack modern, energy-efficient heating, air conditioning, and other appliances.

Don't pay for the building owner's outdated and inefficient heating, air conditioning, and other appliances. Whether you pay for utilities or not, you end up paying extra for these old clinkers.

### ♦ 100   Find an apartment yourself rather than using a broker.

Don't pay someone else to find an apartment for you without first trying it yourself. Check the local newspapers for information on different neighborhoods and drive around the neighborhood you want to live in. Chances are you may find some available apartments or you can deal directly with the superintendent or the building owner. Of course, if the landlord pays the fee to the broker, you won't be out of pocket, but the landlord has probably built the fee into the rent. Rely on yourself first.

### ♦ 101   Demand that interest be paid on your security deposit.

Most of the times the landlord will pay interest on your security deposit—it's the law in many locales. Nevertheless, make sure you are getting a reasonable amount of interest on your security deposit. After all, it's your money.

### ♦ 102   Rent in locales that have rent control or rent stabilization.

If you live in or near a city that has rent control or rent stabilization ordinances, you might as well try to take advantage of them. Learn about the rules and learn how to find one of these deals.

### ♦ 103   Rather than rent a small apartment yourself, rent a larger apartment with a roommate or roommates.

You can get a lot more for your money if you share your space with someone else. Sure, you may prefer to live alone, but the cost of one person in an apartment is becoming prohibitive. At least consider the possibility of sharing an apartment with one or more roommates. You'll get a lot more space in a better building than you would if you went solo.

### ◆ 104 Rent a well-insulated apartment if you have to pay for heat or air conditioning.

Unless you don't have to pay for utilities, rent a unit in a building that is well insulated throughout. Also, drafty old apartments are no fun when the weather is extreme.

### ◆ 105 Don't make improvements to your apartment.

I've never been able to figure out why some people make significant improvements to their apartments at their own expense. Don't enrich your landlord; ask the landlord to make the improvements or, perhaps, to decrease the rent if you do them.

### ◆ 106 If you want to paint or spruce up your apartment, ask the landlord to pay for supplies and/or negotiate a rent reduction.

There's nothing wrong with wanting to spruce up your apartment, but you need to ask the landlord for permission, anyway. Why not ask him or her at least to pay for the supplies for doing his or her work.

### ◆ 107 Take in a roommate.

If your apartment is large enough and/or your financial condition is needful, consider taking in a roommate. This is one of the best ways to save a lot of money quickly. Sure, it's not the best of living arrangements, but if you select carefully, you'll undoubtedly survive the ordeal. In fact, you may enjoy having another person around. I know some people who have shared their apartments very successfully by selecting roommates who travel a lot (e.g., are in the airline business).

### ◆ 108 Spruce up your apartment before you vacate it.

When you move out of your apartment, spend a couple of hours sprucing it up so you can get your deposit back. Don't give the landlord or building superintendent an excuse to refund only partially—or keep outright—your deposit. A couple of hours sweeping the floors, removing some marks on the walls, and sprucing up the kitchen to get your $600 deposit works out to $300 per hour. Not bad at all.

## ♦ 109 Ask for the return of your deposit when you renew your lease.

If you have been a good tenant, why not try to get your deposit back when you renew your lease? This may be a long shot, but it doesn't hurt to try. Perhaps the landlord will return part of it or at least the accrued interest that has been earned on your account.

## ♦ 110 Be a good tenant.

Most landlords prefer a good, stable tenant to receiving ever-increasing rent income in a high-turnover building. Chances are, if you're a good tenant, your rent increase, if any, will be nominal. So avoid the temptation to have a party for five hundred people in your studio, particularly if it's getting close to lease renewal time.

## ♦ 111 Move in with your parents.

If you get along reasonably well with your parents, consider moving back home. If you are young, you will enjoy a much higher standard of living by returning to the homestead than you do now. A word to the wise: Later on in this book I recommend that your parents kick you out of the house to save expenses, so you had best move back in with the express intent of paying your fair share of household expenses.

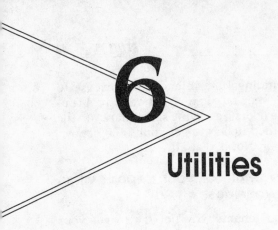

# 6

# Utilities

Do you know that, on average, people spend almost as much on the expenses associated with living in their homes or apartments as they spend on their rent or mortgage? It doesn't matter if your income is $15,000 or $150,000, chances are that you spend a lot of money each year on furnishings, repairs and improvements, insurance, and utilities. In the good old days, utility bills didn't amount to much. Those days are over. Everyone needs to become more energy-conscious. It's better for our environment, our planet, and our wallets—a win-win-win situation. Here are many ways to cut utility bills without sacrificing the comfort to which we have become so accustomed.

♦ **112**  **Keep up-to-date on your local utilities' efforts to reward consumers who cut energy use.**

Many utilities have devised innovative programs that provide financial incentives to their energy-conscious customers. Such rewards include fluorescent light bulb giveaways and free pick up and cash rewards for customers who dispose of inefficient refrigerators, air conditioners, and freezers. Also rebates are offered to utility customers who purchase efficient major appliances.

♦ **113**  **Use the energy-saving services of your local utility.**

Chances are your local utility offers a variety of information and services designed to help you be more energy-efficient.

Take advantage of these free or low-cost services. If it is available in your community, be sure to request an energy audit of your house, and implement its recommendations.

### ◆ 114 Plant trees to save energy.

Plant deciduous trees on the southern and western sides of your home. They will provide needed shade in summer and, in winter, allow the sun to shine through.

### ◆ 115 Replace your smoke alarm batteries at regular intervals.

A properly functioning smoke alarm can save something far more important than mere money—it can save your life and the lives of your loved ones. Make sure your smoke alarms are always working. One convenient way to remember replacing batteries at regular intervals is to replace them twice a year—when you turn your clocks ahead one hour in the spring and back one hour in the fall.

### ◆ 116 Buy energy-efficient light bulbs.

You won't go blind using energy-efficient light bulbs; they're just as bright. Besides, your eyes will take comfort the next time you look at your electricity bill.

### ◆ 117 Make sure light bulbs are the correct wattage for the fixture.

Don't waste energy—or worse—by putting a 100-watt light bulb into a 60-watt fixture.

### ◆ 118 Turn off the lights when you leave the room.

Unless you own stock in the local electric utility, you're not doing your finances any good by leaving lights burning all over your home.

### ◆ 119 Turn off the television when you're not in the room.

If you want to have noise on in the house to keep you company or to fend off burglars, keep the radio on, not the television.

### ◆ 120    Use low-wattage light bulbs.

Remember, when you're replacing light bulbs in your house, you're not lighting up Times Square. Use the minimum wattage that will get the job done, particularly in areas of the house that don't require a lot of light, such as the basement. If the lower-wattage bulb is insufficient, you can always install a higher-wattage bulb.

### ◆ 121    Use fluorescent light bulbs.

Fluorescent light bulbs can replace almost any incandescent bulbs and are much more efficient and long-lasting. If you are skeptical, try them out in a couple of locations in the house. I think you'll be sold on them.

### ◆ 122    Buy appliances with high EERs (energy efficiency ratios).

Opt for appliances with high EERs, even though they may cost a little more. Ultimately you will save money through lower utility bills.

### ◆ 123    Don't set your refrigerator or freezer thermostat too low.

There are a lot of things mentioned in this section of 1001 ways that require a little experimentation. But these experiments often have wonderful outcomes, because you find that you can save a little bit here and a little bit there for many, many years to come. Turn up your refrigerator and freezer thermostats a few degrees and I'll bet you won't know the difference. Check the owner's manual for recommended thermostat settings, but don't take that as gospel. Even if you can raise your thermostat by only a couple of degrees, you'll be saving money.

### ◆ 124    Use a microwave or toaster oven rather than your regular oven.

Unless you're cooking some monstrous item such as your Thanksgiving turkey, you can probably make do very well with either a microwave or toaster oven and use a lot less energy to get the job done.

### ◆ 125   Never run the dishwasher unless it's full.

Your dishwasher doesn't know it's only half filled when it does its thing. Be patient and wait until it's filled to capacity. If you need a particular plate or glass or utensil, don't run the dishwasher, wash it by hand (in cold water).

### ◆ 126   Don't use the heater on your dishwasher.

Many dishwashers have the option of drying your dishes after the washing cycles are completed. I guess if you're too impatient to wait for the dishes to dry naturally, you can have them baked inside the dishwasher. Don't pay dearly for this wasted electricity.

### ◆ 127   Turn off your freezer if you don't store a lot of stuff in it.

One day last year I couldn't find any ice cream in the freezer above the refrigerator, so I went down to the basement to see if there was any in the big freezer. Much to my dismay all I found in there were some ice cubes and a turkey. The ice cubes went in the sink, the turkey went into the freezer compartment of the kitchen refrigerator, and the basement freezer was unplugged. It remains so to this day. If you're not going to make good use of it, don't waste money on an extra freezer.

### ◆ 128   Install surge protectors.

Don't wait to find out the expensive damage that lightning can cause to your appliances. Have a professional install a surge protector for the entire home, or you can install surge protectors designed for individual outlets.

### ◆ 129   Use appliances when electricity rates are lower.

Some utilities charge less for electricity in off-peak hours. If this pertains to you, plan to use your electric appliances, including the washing machine, dryer, and dishwasher during off-peak hours. If you can do some cooking then, too, all the better.

### ♦ 130 Don't use the dryer if you've washed just a few items.

Unless you need to wear them right away, if you've washed just a few items of clothing, hang them up to dry rather than wasting money by running the dryer. By the way, always keep a few spare hangers "hanging around" the washing machine to use when necessary.

### ♦ 131 Dry two loads of laundry at once.

Try to plan your washing and drying endeavors so you can dry more than one load of laundry at the same time. Your dryer is one of the biggest energy users in your house. The less you use it, the better.

### ♦ 132 Use cold-water detergent for clothes washing.

Are you one of those who think that clothes have to be scalded to be clean? Why don't you at least give cold water washing a try? It may not work for all of your clothes, but if it works for some of them, you'll be able to cut your electricity bill.

### ♦ 133 Use fewer cycles when running the dishwasher.

Your dishwasher probably offers the option of a variety of cycles. Of course, the more cycles, the greater the amount of water and electricity used. Try running the dishwasher on fewer cycles. Your dishes may come out perfectly clean, and fewer cycles means more money for you.

### ♦ 134 Don't overuse hot water.

Whenever you turn on the hot water, just imagine a cash register opening up to receive a steady flow of your hard-earned money. Too many times a day, people use hot water when cold or warm water will do just as well.

### ◆ 135 Buy a water saver for your shower.

You probably can pick up a water saver free from a local utility. You won't even know the difference after you install it.

### ◆ 136 Install a single-control shower valve.

Single-control shower valves let you preset the water temperature. It saves the water wasted (not to mention the discomfort) while you make hot and cold adjustments with two separate valves.

### ◆ 137 Turn down the temperature on your hot-water heater.

You may well be able to make do with a lower temperature on your hot-water heater. See if you can live with it ten degrees lower. If so, reduce it some more. Lowering the temperature a few degrees can add up to energy-saving dollars.

### ◆ 138 Turn off your hot-water heater while away from home for an extended period.

If the house is empty for an extended period of time—say, a vacation—why do you need your hot-water heater working morning, noon, and night keeping the water hot? Turn it off.

### ◆ 139 Wrap your hot-water heater.

Buy a coat for your hot-water heater. It will thank you with lower heating bills.

### ◆ 140 Install a hot-water-heater timer control.

Your faithful hot-water heater stands ready to deliver *agua caliente*. You're darn glad of that at seven in the morning. But is it really necessary to have 120-degree water at the ready in the middle of the night or during the day if no one is at home?

A timer control will let you have hot water when you need it, but you won't be paying for the privilege of having it when you don't.

### ◆ 141   Insulate hot-water pipes.

A lot of heat is lost when your hot water snakes its way from heater to faucet. It's easy and inexpensive to insulate those pipes. The result: You'll get hot water quicker and cheaper.

### ◆ 142   Install aerators on all faucets.

Aerators are another simple, moneysaving device that everyone should have.

### ◆ 143   Don't fall for water purification sales pitches.

You may well know the routine. Someone comes in to test your water, and they find so many alien bodies in it that it's frankly unbelievable that you and your family have lived this long. Of course, "your problems can be solved," so they say, with a water purification system—and an expensive one, at that. It is far better for you to have your water tested independently. If you need purer water, you can select your own system *sans* sales pitch and can save several hundred dollars in the process.

### ◆ 144   Lower the water level of your toilet.

Toilets waste a lot of water. Fiddle around with the float in the back of the toilet so it lowers the water level a bit. You'll either have to bend the rod or use a screwdriver; you can manage it without having to call in your plumber. He's probably off vacationing at his condo on the French Riviera, anyway. Lowering the water level a little can save you a lot over the course of a year.

### ◆ 145   Buy a shallow-trap toilet.

Next time you need to purchase or replace a potty (as it is known in the Pond household), buy a shallow-trap toilet, which uses less water per flush.

## ◆ 146    Fix dripping faucets.

Don't put off fixing a dripping faucet, especially if it's dripping hot water. Nine times out of ten you can fix it.

## ◆ 147    Fix a constantly running toilet.

A constantly running toilet wastes an unbelievable amount of water. You can probably fix it yourself. Check a home repair manual.

## ◆ 148    Keep your sump pump in good working order.

Unless you've always wanted a swimming pool in your basement, clean and inspect your sump pump at least annually. Test the operation of the pump more often—at least every three months.

## ◆ 149    Water your lawn at night.

You'll get many more miles per gallon by watering your lawn at night than you will during the day, when what we try to throw on the lawn evaporates.

## ◆ 150    Fix a "leaky" house.

It doesn't necessarily cost a fortune to fix a drafty dwelling. Make your home weathertight unless you have an obsessive desire to heat or cool the outdoors. Insulation, caulking, and weatherstripping—all of which you can probably do yourself—will decrease the amount you have to shell out each month for heating and air conditioning.

## ◆ 151    Insulate your attic.

Be sure your attic and any floors over unheated spaces are adequately insulated. It's usually an easy do-it-yourself project that can save some serious money.

## ◆ 152    Use insulated window treatments (shades/drapes).

There's no longer a requirement that insulated shades and draperies have to be ugly. People who have installed insulated window treatments swear by them, so consider this energy-saving investment.

### ◆ 153 Add more insulation.

You already have insulation? You'll probably benefit from adding more. Check out what you have, and speak with your local utility about how much you should have. Then try doing it yourself.

### ◆ 154 Check to see if you are eligible for state income-tax credits for installing energy-saving devices in your home.

Some states provide income-tax credits or deductions for taxpayers who take certain energy-conservation measures. Be sure to check your state tax regulations to see if these tax incentives are available.

### ◆ 155 Put on an extra sweater, and turn down the heat.

Sweaters are a lot cheaper than oil, natural gas, or electricity. They're also better-looking.

### ◆ 156 Size up your air-conditioning needs carefully.

Under- or overestimating the amount of air conditioning you need are both expensive mistakes. Too much air conditioning will cycle excessively, causing inefficient operation and a shorter running life. Too little air conditioning can be uncomfortable and can also shorten running life. Your air-conditioning dealer will assist you in making the sizing calculations.

### ◆ 157 Room air conditioners may be cheaper than central air conditioning.

While central air conditioning is usually thought to be preferable, room air conditioners can actually be more energy-efficient from both a cost and a comfort standpoint. You can operate them only in rooms that are being used. So before

taking the plunge to installing central air conditioning, see if
you might be able to get by with window units.

### ♦ 158  Turn down the air conditioning.

Save a lot of money by running the air conditioner less. In
many areas, fans make sense (except on the hottest days).

### ♦ 159  Turn down the heat or air conditioning in rooms you don't use regularly.

It's kind of silly to heat or air-condition a rarely used room.
If you can, reduce or turn off the heat or air conditioning in
unused rooms. Take a lesson from the many frugal New
Englanders who close down several rooms in their homes
during the winter so they don't have to waste money heating
them.

### ♦ 160  Install a zoned heating and/or air-conditioning system.

A zoned heating and/or air-conditioning system can save a lot
of energy money by heating or cooling only those areas of the
house occupied rather than the whole house. If you're changing your heating and/or air conditioning, check out a zoned
system.

### ♦ 161  Use fans instead of air conditioners.

Certainly there will be days when you would love to have air
conditioning, but they're usually few in number. You could
always go to a movie or inexpensive restaurant to cool down.
Even in hotter climes, those who want to reduce their energy
costs—and who doesn't?—will often install an attic fan in
addition to the air conditioners. Such fans can be used on
warm days and spare the need for constant air conditioning.

### ♦ 162  Install heat reflectors on the back of your radiators.

The wall behind your radiator is not desperate for heat, so
buy or make a heat reflector for each radiator.

### ♦ 163 Have your heating and air-conditioning systems cleaned and inspected every year.

Don't let an inefficient heating and/or air-conditioning system drive up your utility bills. Pay a little money to have them cleaned and inspected each year. A small investment now will pay for itself many times over when those electricity and fuel bills come rolling in.

### ♦ 164 Install a programmable thermostat.

Another project you can probably do yourself, and the savings can be dramatic. Quite simply, a programmable thermostat allows you to automatically change the thermostat setting when the house is empty or the family's asleep, because it's kind of silly to use up heat when the family is either absent or unconscious.

### ♦ 165 Consider heating with wood or coal.

You can probably get a lot more heat for your money with wood or coal than you can with electricity, oil, or gas. The newer wood-burning and coal-burning stoves are very efficient, so whether you supplement your existing heating system or replace your central heating system with a wood-burning or coal-burning stove, it's well worth considering.

### ♦ 166 Use shades and draperies to reduce heating and cooling costs.

If it's warm outside, close your shades and draperies on the sunny side, then open them at night. In the winter, keep the sunny side open during daylight and closed at night. These simple tasks will lower your heating and cooling costs.

### ♦ 167 Don't leave your fireplace damper open (unless there's a fire in the fireplace).

Remember to close your fireplace damper. I don't like to think of the number of times I have neglected to close the fireplace damper long after the fire was out. I bought a brass plaque that hangs from the fireplace and reads "damper open" on one side and "damper closed" on the other as a reminder. My two-year-old loves to flip it back and forth, so the plaque doesn't do much good. I hope you can do a better job than the Pond family at keeping your fireplace damper closed.

## ◆ 168  Use the smaller burners on your stove.

Most stove-top cooking jobs can be done over the smaller burners. Smaller burners and smaller pots mean smaller gas or electricity bills.

## ◆ 169  Buy, don't rent telephones.

Perfectly good telephones can be bought for a pittance, so why rent them? Don't buy the argument that by renting them they will be repaired at no cost. If your store-bought telephone breaks, you can get it repaired inexpensively, or you can buy another one.

## ◆ 170  Make your long-distance calls at night and on weekends.

Some people think that since long-distance rates drop all the time they can afford the luxury of calling whenever the mood strikes them. The cheapest times to call are typically between 11:00 P.M. and 8:00 A.M. each night and morning, all day Saturday, and all day Sunday except from 5:00 P.M. to 11:00 P.M. You can save a lot, particularly if you talk a lot.

## ◆ 171  Scrutinize your phone bill.

Make sure you aren't paying for someone else's phone calls. Review every phone bill. (It's also a convenient way to find an excuse to start an argument with your spouse or partner: "How can you possibly spend forty-two minutes talking with your mother?")

## ◆ 172  Use the phone book before calling directory assistance.

Directory assistance can cost big money! Check your phone bills to see how much you use directory assistance. I've never been able to figure out why some people are too lazy to look it up in the phone book.

### ♦ 173 Keep an up-to-date address book with telephone numbers.

Did you know that you pay for directory assistance calls in most areas of the country? By keeping an up-to-date address book handy, you should rarely need to use (and pay for) directory assistance.

### ♦ 174 Avoid making credit card telephone calls.

Telephone credit cards are handy, but you pay dearly for the convenience. Don't get into the habit of making credit card calls unless, of course, they are business-related and your company pays for them.

### ♦ 175 Write down things you want to talk about on the telephone before you call.

Here's the typical scenario: You call a loved one, have a pleasant conversation, but spend the last two or three minutes of the call trying to remember something important that you wanted to discuss. Finally you bid *adieu* without remembering what you wanted to talk about in the first place. After hanging up, you go nuts trying to recall what it was, and then—"aha!"—it suddenly comes back to you. What do you do? You call back. This type of situation, which you may well repeat time after time, could be easily eliminated by jotting down a few notes *before* you make your next long-distance phone call. You save money and avoid frustration.

### ♦ 176 Eliminate unneeded extras on your phone service.

Many people don't even know what optional extras they have on their phone service. Do you really need call forwarding, call waiting, and speed dialing? They cost just a few dollars a month, which means that over the years they cost a few hundred dollars. Check to see what you've got—if you don't know—and drop unneeded extras.

### ♦ 177    Suspend telephone service if away from home for an extended period.

You may be able to save a few dollars by suspending your telephone service if you're away for a few months or on vacation or an extended business trip. Check with the phone company for particulars.

### ♦ 178    Don't answer your phone during the early evening.

Don't answer the telephone in the early evening, because it will almost certainly be some salesperson trying to convince you to buy something you can get along without.

### ♦ 179    Pay your utility bills in person.

A lot of utilities allow you to pay your utility bills at a local store or some other convenient location. If you happen to be at that location, bring your utility bills with you. The savings, the price of a stamp for each utility bill you pay in person, are modest, but they are savings nonetheless.

# III

# SHOPPING

# Food

While you may not think it's possible, one of the easiest ways to reduce your living expenses is to become a wiser and more selective food shopper and mealmaker. There are numerous opportunities to save. Whether you're planning a grocery shopping trip, pushing the cart through the aisles, or preparing meals in your kitchen, the following gastronomic guidelines will help you trim your family budget.

### ◆ 180 Clip and use coupons.

You'll be amazed how those nickels and dimes add up. Some coupon experts save hundreds of dollars per year on groceries.

### ◆ 181 Shop on "double coupon days."

If you're a coupon user—and you should be—do your shopping on "double coupon days" if you can. Some grocers even offer "triple coupon days." If the trend continues, maybe they'll have free groceries. I doubt it.

### ◆ 182 Even though coupons look like a bargain, you may be able to buy other brands for less.

Generally, coupons are a great way to save money. But smart shoppers check the prices of other brands, including generic brands, to see if they can beat the price of the "couponed" items.

### ♦ 183 Don't buy something just because you have a coupon.

Whatever you're buying—food, hardware, lawn fertilizer, clothing, it doesn't matter—you should buy only what you're going to use. Sometimes you may be tempted to buy something just because you have a coupon—I mean, a bargain is a bargain. But a bargain becomes a waste of money if you really don't need the item.

### ♦ 184 Check the newspaper or circulars for items on sale at the supermarket.

Be sure to review newspapers and any circulars that come your way for sale items. Also, when you go to the store, be sure to look at the sale items posted on the store's windows and in its aisles.

### ♦ 185 Don't go shopping too frequently.

Try to organize your grocery shopping expeditions so that you're not forever making trips to buy just a few items. It wastes gas and it probably wastes grocery money because you'll be tempted to go to the convenience store if you need only a few items.

### ♦ 186 Avoid shopping at convenience stores.

Unless you prefer to pay outrageous prices, do your grocery shopping at the grocery store. You'll save money on food, and you'll avoid the tempting lottery machine.

### ♦ 187 Never go grocery shopping on an empty stomach.

This is an inviolable law. You'll buy fewer groceries, and you won't risk serious physical injury from trying to carry five hundred pounds of groceries into your kitchen.

### ♦ 188 Don't bring your spouse food shopping if you're going to shop wisely.

They are more likely to impede your shopping by questioning items in the cart or going off on their own selecting unneeded or overpriced products. If they insist on going, tell them to sit in the car.

### ◆ 189 Don't bring your children food shopping.

They will pull things off the shelf, insist on your buying junk food, and do the standard crying and running through the aisles. The result: your little angels so distract you from the serious business at hand—making the most of your grocery dollar—that the expedition is almost bound to cost you more than it would have had you shopped solo.

### ◆ 190 Bring your own bags to the grocery store.

If your grocery store is one of the many that now charges for grocery bags, nip that needless expense in the bud by bringing your own.

### ◆ 191 Shop at food warehouses instead of supermarkets.

Some grocery stores are cheaper than others, and food warehouses are often the cheapest of all.

### ◆ 192 Buy in bulk quantities, but only if you'll use it all.

True, it's more expensive up front to buy in bulk, but it's a great way to save on staples and dry goods.

### ◆ 193 Buy generic groceries.

You probably think that generic groceries are inherently inferior. Have you tried them? You can always go back to wasting your money on more expensive brands if your taste buds are offended.

### ◆ 194 Buy store brand products.

You'll find a lot of store brands available that are just as good as the heavily marketed brands, but you won't have to pay for the advertising.

◆ **195** Return your bottles and cans so you can get your deposit back.

Sure it's inconvenient, but you're making a trip to the grocery store anyway, and they add up over time. Do you realize that if you returned twenty million cans at a nickel apiece, you'd be a millionaire?

◆ **196** Buy soft drinks in large bottles.

If you buy soft drinks in large bottles, you get a lot more for your money and you usually wind up wasting less. The twelve-ounce cans are more convenient, but you pay a lot for this convenience. Also, how many times have you ended up throwing out part of an unfinished twelve-ounce soft-drink can? This shouldn't happen if you pour a reasonable portion out of a large bottle.

◆ **197** Find the best buys at the grocery store by comparing the unit prices.

You no longer need to be a mathematics genius to find the best buys, and thank heaven for that, because otherwise the consumer doesn't stand a chance against the ingenious ways that manufacturers use to put a small quantity of product into a large package. Get into the habit of checking unit prices and you'll get a lot more for your dollar. Also, if you shop at more than one store, note the unit prices of some items that you purchase frequently and compare them between or among the stores.

◆ **198** Always check the "reduced" section of the grocery store.

Don't turn up your nose at the reduced-price section of the grocery store. This is where they put packaged goods that are slightly askew, day-old bakery items, etc. Always look. If there's something you need there, check out its condition. If it passes muster (don't be too choosy), buy it.

◆ **199** Buy perishable items in season.

Don't buy frozen corn when corn on the cob is in season. Enjoy fresh, seasonal food at very reasonable prices.

◆ **200** **Get some exercise at the grocery store.**

Look for items that are on the bottom or top shelves. High-ticket items are usually placed at eye level.

◆ **201** **Check the expiration date on milk and milk products.**

Avoid items with dates about to expire.

◆ **202** **Ditto for perishables such as poultry.**

Don't buy perishables that are going to reach their expiration dates before you intend to use them. The last thing you want to do is throw out what would have been perfectly good food.

◆ **203** **Avoid buying foods that are packaged together when they can be purchased separately for less.**

You *pay* for the convenience of packaging that combines food items that you probably already have or that can be purchased separately for a lot less money. You either have to be incorrigibly lazy or incredibly rich to be able to afford to make a habit of buying such items.

◆ **204** **Don't pay extra for extra ingredients.**

Paying for soap with moisturizer, for example, or cereal with raisins is almost always considerably more expensive than buying soap and moisturizer or cereal and raisins separately. There are never enough raisins in the cereal with raisins anyway.

◆ **205** **Avoid buying "single servings."**

Single servings are another one of those supposedly convenient food items that you pay dearly for. Prepare for a shock when you compare the unit pricing for single servings versus a larger-size package.

### ◆ 206 Buy produce by the bag rather than individually.

Sure, the potatoes or tomatoes or whatever that are artfully stacked in the produce section look marvelous, but you'll almost always save by buying produce by the bag rather than selecting each individual item and bagging it yourself. Yes, the potatoes may not be quite as large or quite as handsome when they're in a ten-pound bag, but since when do you buy food on the basis of its beauty?

### ◆ 207 Don't pay the store to put the finishing touches on your produce.

Is it really worth the substantial extra cost to buy produce that has been bisected, dissected, or otherwise made more useful when you could do the same yourself?

### ◆ 208 Buy orange juice concentrate in the frozen-food section rather than by the carton.

Most of the orange juice you buy by the carton is made from concentrate anyway, so why don't you do it yourself by buying the frozen concentrate? If you're a big orange juice family, the savings could be substantial.

### ◆ 209 Shop for substitutes for baby food.

Prepackaged baby food is certainly convenient and is certainly expensive. After checking with your baby's pediatrician, learn how to make your own baby food. You might first buy a book on the subject.

### ◆ 210 Compare the prices on nonfood items available at the supermarket with the same items at other stores.

All the nonfood items the supermarkets carry are certainly a convenience if they avoid an additional trip to the drugstore, department store, or florist. But you may be paying more for these items at the supermarket than you would at other stores. Compare prices before making a habit of buying non-food items at the supermarket.

### ◆ 211 Cook your own food rather than buying prepared food.

Cooking your own food is more nutritious and less expensive than prepared food, and the food is tastier. What additional arguments do you need?

### ◆ 212 Store leftovers—don't waste food.

But be careful: Long-kept leftovers may cost you in doctor's bills.

### ◆ 213 Get creative with leftovers.

Take the attitude that something can always be made of leftovers. Why not experiment so you can find new uses for last week's or last month's uneaten but still edible food?

### ◆ 214 Go through your food cabinets periodically to make sure you're using canned and packaged foods before their expiration dates.

It's really a shame to have to throw out what was perfectly good canned or packaged food because the expiration dates are past. It's also inexcusable. Go through your food cabinets every few months and display those items whose expiration dates are nearing so you'll remember to use them.

### ◆ 215 Double-check your inventory before going grocery shopping.

Don't rely on your memory when selecting items at the grocery store. Before you leave to go shopping, check the items on your list against your food inventory. In that way you'll avoid buying something you have plenty of. (Hint: You probably have enough salad dressing to last you fifteen years.)

◆ **216** **Grow your own vegetables.**

Even if you have a small lot, there's no reason why you can't grow your own crops. If you're skeptical, start with a small plot. If you like the results of your initial planting, you can always expand your farm.

◆ **217** **Grow your own spices on a windowsill.**

Home owners and apartment owners alike can set up their own spice farm on a windowsill. It's fun, inexpensive, and you'll love the satisfaction of using your homegrown spices.

◆ **218** **Watch your weight.**

If you think gaining weight is expensive, try dieting.

◆ **219** **Spend a stamp to take advantage of manufacturers' rebates.**

Unless the amount of the refund is less than the cost of a stamp and an envelope, send for the rebate.

# 8

## CLOTHING

Are you a clotheshorse? Let's face it: There's a lot to be said for nice clothing. It makes us look good (or so we think), and we feel better about ourselves when we're decked out in sartorial finery. But alas, it's far too easy to go overboard on clothing. Madison Avenue is the culprit. After all, if you don't keep up with the latest fashion, you're out of it. But if you're too practical to fall for the "fashion line," you're well on your way to cutting your clothing expenses.

If you want to look your best—and who doesn't?—you have two choices: You can spend a king's ransom on a nice wardrobe, or you can spend a lot less on a nice wardrobe. The choice is yours. The following tips will help you dress up without denuding your checking account.

### ◆ 220  Take advantage of bargains and sales when you need an item.

Remember Pond's maxim: You never save money when you buy something on sale. You've spent money. However, if you genuinely need that frock, by all means buy it when it goes on sale. In fact, almost every item of clothing known to mankind eventually goes on sale. The problem that we all have, however, is that when something goes on sale, we automatically think we need it. 'Tain't necessarily so.

### ◆ 221  Buy at discount clothing centers.

You'll be surprised how many of your better-dressed acquaintances aren't paying full price for their perfectly good clothes.

They probably won't admit it, but they're addicted to discount clothing stores—marvelous things to get hooked on.

### ◆ 222  Buy clothes off-season.

With a little foresight, you can save a lot on your clothing bill by buying suits, overcoats, etc., off-season. The last thing a clothing retailer wants is to carry a heavy wool overcoat into the spring season. You can alleviate your retailer's misery by taking that coat off his hands in April—at a hefty discount from what less thrifty customers paid only a couple of months earlier.

### ◆ 223  Find out when the store is going to have a sale on clothing you need.

If you've been snooping around the clothing racks and find some threads you want desperately to purchase, first ask the salesperson if there's any likelihood that these items are going to go on sale in the near future. I've found that they're very forthright on this, and waiting a few weeks to indulge my sartorial cravings has saved me a lot of money over the years.

### ◆ 224  Stock up on necessaries during seasonal sales.

Each season, many stores put most of their stock on sale. While we often hightail it to the store to buy some high-ticket item that's 40 percent off (which we probably don't need), we pass right by the sock, hosiery, or underwear counters, which also offer good discounts. You probably thought that there were only two things certain in life: death and taxes. But there's a third certainty: You're going to need to buy skivvies and socks/hosiery. Since the stuff goes on sale a few times a year, there is no reason to pay retail for these necessaries. Stock up when they're on sale.

### ◆ 225  Get on the store's mailing list so you will be informed in advance of sales.

A lot of apparel and department stores let their "best" customers in on the sales before they're announced to the public.

Do you have to spend a fortune at the store to become a best customer? Of course not. Ask a clerk. Chances are they'll be more than happy to put you on the store's mailing list.

### ◆ 226 Inspect clothing carefully before purchasing it.

It's hard-earned money that you're plunking down on your new clothing. Spend a couple of minutes going over the garment to make sure it has been properly put together and that it's all there. In that way you'll avoid finding out there's a problem when you get your garment home, or worse, when you find that seam in your dress has a gaping hole in it just after you've been seated at the White House dinner. (Don't laugh—if you follow the advice in this book, you may well become so rich that the president will just *have* to have you dine regularly at the White House. Haven't you noticed how much our presidents love to surround themselves with rich people?)

### ◆ 227 Buy used clothing.

Hold on a minute. You probably think used clothing is reserved only for the "down and out." Nay, nay. You'll be surprised at what you can find at stores selling "pre-owned" clothes. Many cities have several secondhand clothing stores that cater to the carriage trade. After all, many rich folks think nothing of discarding their clothing after it's barely used. I've known some genuine fashion plates who wouldn't think of buying new. Check some of these stores out. You have nothing to lose, and I'll bet you'll be pleasantly surprised at what you'll find. You can also get some super used clothing for children. After all, kids grow like bamboo, so they never wear out good-quality clothing. That's why you find a lot of it in the secondhand clothing stores.

### ◆ 228 Buy wash-and-wear.

Unless you have a laundress, or you love to iron, you should opt for wash-and-wear clothing. True, all-natural fiber clothing is the "in" thing, but unless you own a dry-cleaning establishment, you're going to spend a lot of money maintaining them. If you love natural fiber clothing, why don't you still buy some wash-and-wear for everyday use? Then you can save your natural fiber clothing for special occasions.

## ◆ 229 Buy medium-weight clothes that you can wear (almost) year-round.

If you live in an area of the country that has seasons, you get to enjoy a varied climate, but you pay dearly for it, since you have to maintain both a heavier weight and a lightweight wardrobe. Rather than stocking up on two different wardrobes, which your clothier would love you to do, try "midweight" clothing. The manufacturers claim that you can wear these clothes ten months a year (they don't tell you which ten, however). I love this clothing, and I've found that if it can be worn ten months of the year it can really be worn twelve. Sure, there are a couple of days in the summer when it's too hot and a few days in the winter when I wish I were wearing something a bit heavier, but I am comforted by the amount of money I'm saving by not having two complete wardrobes.

## ◆ 230 Buy clothes that complement other clothing or accessories you already have.

Always remember what you have in your clothing larder before you purchase another article of clothing. You can really dig a financial hole for yourself buying some nice item only to find that you now need a shirt or blouse to match it because you don't have anything at home or because your jewelry just doesn't go with this outfit so you've got to buy more jewelry.

## ◆ 231 Buy suits with two pairs of pants, since the pants wear out first.

Men: when was the last time your suit jacket wore out before the pants? If you wear suits a lot, try to purchase suits with two pairs of pants. Sometimes you can order a separate pair of pants through the retailer. Some clothing stores now offer the option of a second pair of pants with a suit, which, in effect, means you will probably get twice as much use out of the suit for far less than twice the price of a one-pants suit.

## ◆ 232 Look for "irregular" or "imperfect" clothing.

Just as some people are pros at assembling marvelous wardrobes out of secondhand clothing, so others are experts at buying "seconds." How do they, and how can you, do it? Simply inspect the clothing carefully before you buy it. Find out why it is not of first quality. Often the problem is either imperceptible or easily correctable, in which case you've gotten a perfectly good article of clothing for a song.

## ◆ 233 Stay away from designer labels on everything from clothes to cosmetics.

No wonder clothing designers and cosmetics mavens live in baronial splendor. Have you seen how much they charge for their products? Believe me, eschewing these overpriced products will not consign you to a life of ill-clad ugliness. Remember, ostentation is *out* in the 1990s.

## ◆ 234 Buy classic clothing.

Try not to get caught up in the expensive hysteria of owning the latest fashions. If you do so, you're going to find that the Madison Avenue crowd has got you where they want you. Thanks to them the superfashionable clothes you buy this year will be either dowdy or gaudy next year. Smart (and well-dressed) consumers buy classic clothing like Brooks Brothers suits—apparel that looks good year in and year out. Sure, they may want to buy an occasional outfit that is avant-garde, but their closets mostly contain well-crafted, attractive clothing and accessories that can be worn and admired for years to come.

## ◆ 235 Join a club for frequent underwear purchasers.

Many department stores have "clubs" that reward frequent purchases of hosiery and underwear with freebies after you've purchased several items.

## ◆ 236   Find a good tailor.

Do you buy new clothes when you still have clothes whose lapels are too wide or whose hemlines are too long? Ask your tailor to take them in or take it up. It'll be like buying a new item for the cost of the alteration.

## ◆ 237   Find a good dry cleaner.

It's amazing how many people will put up with cleaners who burn their shirts or break their buttons. Believe it or not, it is possible to have your shirts laundered properly if you must have your shirts laundered. Why pay to have them ruined?

## ◆ 238   Cut down on your dry cleaning.

Don't take your clothes to be dry-cleaned just because they're wrinkled. Opt for "press only," or better yet, iron them yourself.

## ◆ 239   Don't let your weight fluctuate.

I've been fighting a long—and losing—battle with my waistline over the years. Weight gain or loss can be very expensive when it comes to clothing. First, the tailor alters the clothing to fit my changed dimensions, but eventually the dimensions change more than the clothing can, so it's off to the clothier for new threads. If you've been through this, you know how expensive it can be. So don't let your weight fluctuate—it's better for both your physical and financial health.

## ◆ 240   If you've gained weight that you recently lost (or, better, lost weight that you recently gained), check your old clothes before going out to buy new ones.

If your weight fluctuates, you may well have three sets of clothing of different sizes (e.g., fat, medium, and thin). So if you are a "new size," check the closet out before going on a buying rampage. There may be some perfectly good clothes there that will fit you (again).

♦ **241** **Find a good cobbler.**

Fix your old shoes before buying new ones. While you are in the cobbler's shop, be sure to ask him about preventive steps you can take to keep your shoes from wearing down and wearing out.

♦ **242** **Put rubber heels on your shoes.**

I've heard some people say that they get leather heels on their shoes because leather looks better than rubber. What do these people do, walk on their hands? Rubber heels last far longer than leather, and you get better traction, which might save some medical bills someday.

♦ **243** **Replace broken or lost buttons promptly.**

All it takes is one broken or lost button to put an article of clothing out of action. Sometimes it might even provide you with an excuse to replace the article of clothing when it is so simple to replace the button. If it's an unusual button, check with your local fabric store or tailor for a replacement. If necessary, change all the buttons, but keep your clothing in good working order.

♦ **244** **Put patches on the elbows of your sport coat when they wear out instead of discarding it.**

Only your tailor will know for sure that you're recycling an otherwise worthless sport coat. After all, some new sport coats come with elbow patches. You'll also look very professorial. Perhaps your sport coat will even get you a part-time position teaching at the local community college.

♦ **245** **Launder your own shirts.**

If you wear shirts or blouses that have to be ironed and you send them out, it could easily cost you $390 per year (5 shirts per week x $1.50 per shirt x 52 weeks). No wonder my dry cleaner drives a Cadillac. Consider doing your shirts yourself, because $390 is a lot of money.

## ◆ 246   Rent formal wear rather than buy.

Unless you're some sort of social butterfly who is always donning tailcoats, tuxedos, or ball gowns, you really shouldn't buy formal wear when it's so easy to rent. If you have just been invited to a formal affair—the first one in five years—don't delude yourself into thinking that you've been transformed into a member of that long-since-vanished Cole Porter/Fred Astair café society and end up spending two weeks' pay on drop-dead formal regalia. Rent it instead. No one will suspect, and I'll wager you'll look pretty snappy in your hired soup and fish.

## ◆ 247   Wear old clothes and shoes around the house or yard rather than discarding them.

Unless you're expecting a *60 Minutes* film crew to be showing up at your front door, there's no reason to bedeck yourself in sartorial splendor when you're on your home turf. Get every last bit of use out of your clothes and shoes. Another benefit: When somebody comes to your door soliciting a donation, one look at you in yesteryear's clothes will have them believing that *you* need the donation.

## ◆ 248   Recycle knee-high socks into ankle-length.

When the heels and toes of your knee-high socks are worn through, cut off the foot portion, round out the front for toes, and you've got a usable pair of ankle-length socks.

## ◆ 249   Use discarded clothing as cleaning or dust cloths.

The usefulness of your clothing doesn't end when you can't wear it anymore. I find that I wear a lot of my shirts, etc., to the point where they are so worn out that I can't in good conscience donate them to the Salvation Army or Goodwill Industries. So these shirts become washable cleaning cloths that provide many additional months of service. My old shirts and underwear virtually eliminate the need to buy those expensive all-purpose household wiping cloths.

# 9

# Other Necessaries and Not-So-Necessaries

**W**e all love to shop. It is one of life's great pleasures. Unfortunately, many of us end up getting too much pleasure from shopping—which is detrimental to our financial health. This chapter provides lots of suggestions for getting the most for your hard-earned money. It will help you maximize your dollars' value when buying things you absolutely need. Also, it will help you restrain those impulses we all have—the ones that tell us we absolutely need something we don't *really* need.

### ◆ 250 Just because you're going shopping doesn't mean you have to buy something.

You don't have to be overjoyed if you come back from a shopping sojourn empty-handed, but don't get depressed about it, either. If you're a wise shopper, and you don't find something you need that's reasonably priced, there's no need to buy anything. Actually, if you have resisted the temptation, why don't you treat yourself to an ice cream cone or some other inexpensive reward? Your good judgment is good cause for a modest celebration.

### ◆ 251 Be patient. Everything eventually goes on sale.

One of the problems we all share is that spending money feels good, and when we want something, we want it now. But if you can postpone both gratifications, chances are the item will still be there, on sale. You can save a lot of money over the years if you recognize that the item you so desperately want to purchase now will probably go on sale in the end.

## ◆ 252  Shop with a budget. Stick to it.

Most of us go off to buy something saying, "I'm not going to spend any more than $100." And most of us come back having spent $139 or $195. True, your budget may have been unrealistically low, but it is far more likely that you ended up buying something fancier than you needed. One way to stick to your budget is to let the salesperson know your limit. Who knows? He or she may lower the price a little bit if you're adamant. On the other hand, if the salesperson tells you that your budget is unrealistic, go to another store.

## ◆ 253  Take advantage of bargains and sales when you need an item.

The problem, of course, is that when we see something on sale, we automatically assume we need it. If you genuinely need something, by all means try to purchase it at the lowest price.

## ◆ 254  Check your newspaper for great deals on used furniture.

Get some amazing bargains by buying used furniture through the newspaper. Hint: In responding to the ad, find out where the seller lives. If it's a fancy neighborhood, get there fast.

## ◆ 255  Bargain with vendors.

If you're buying something you think is too expensive or a little over your budget, don't hesitate to bargain. You may be pleasantly surprised to find that there is some give in the selling price, particularly for higher-ticket items.

## ◆ 256  Shop for major purchases late in the month.

You may be able to strike a better deal on a major purchase such as an appliance by shopping just before the end of the month. Many retailers are anxious to meet their monthly sales quotas, and some will be ready to bargain to make an additional sale.

### ♦ 257   Buy floor models.

Save money by buying a floor model of an appliance or piece of furniture or whatever. Of course, you must carefully inspect and be prepared to reject any of them. Also, be sure to point out any obvious flaws in the floor model to strike an even better bargain. Don't shy away from something that has a few scratches. (You'll probably get a few scratches on something you buy new after it's been in the house a couple of weeks.) Finally, if applicable, find out what kind of warranty you'll be entitled to.

### ♦ 258   Buy "seconds."

Most people are aware of "seconds" when it comes to clothing, but a variety of other products are available at a substantially reduced price even though they're slightly damaged or otherwise defective. It doesn't hurt to ask, and any store should tell you straight out what's wrong with the item. You may surprise yourself with a good bargain even though it might require a little touch-up when you get it home.

### ♦ 259   Always prepare a list before you go shopping, and resist impulse purchases.

Most people prepare a list before grocery shopping. They should do the same when going off to a department store, hardware store, or on any other shopping expedition. Armed with the list, you can go about your appointed rounds without being distracted by all the other goodies that tempt your pocketbook. Be strong, stick to your list, and resist purchasing anything on impulse.

### ♦ 260   Compare in-store prices with those in mail-order catalogs.

You may be able to buy appliances, clothing, and any number of other items by mail for less than you can at the local store.

True, you don't get the immediate gratification of being able to schlepp the item home right after buying it, but if you can save money by waiting for a few days or a couple of weeks, isn't it worth it?

## ♦ 261 Don't shop at the last minute.

One of the worst shopping mistakes is to wait until you have no choice but to purchase the item. Whether your sense of urgency is actual or just imagined, you'll go into the store with the attitude that price is no object. (The salespeople will absolutely love you.) So heed the following rule of thumb: The more expensive the item, the longer you should plan ahead to purchase it.

## ♦ 262 Don't drive by factory outlets without stopping in.

It's a shame to pass by a factory outlet. You may find a genuine bargain there if, and only if, you need the item.

## ♦ 263 Join a buying club.

Buying clubs are not tough to join. You don't have to be a member of the Social Register, nor do you have to provide five letters of recommendation. Instead, you pay a small annual membership fee, which allows you to purchase goods at discounted prices. Sometimes you have to be an employee of a certain organization, government unit, or credit union, but what buying clubs lack in amenities—and the warehouse-like atmosphere certainly lacks some amenities—they more than make up for in good prices. Check them out.

## ♦ 264 Don't shop via television.

Television shopping networks are a big and growing business in this country. Unfortunately, some people become addicted to them, and usually it's the people who can least afford them. Home television shopping is the ultimate channel for the impulse purchaser. If you find something that really strikes your fancy, okay; but you probably aren't getting the bargain you think you are. Don't get into the expensive habit of buying via television.

## ◆ 265  Buy in bulk quantities, but only if you'll use it all.

Buying in bulk is a great way to cut down costs on household items you use a lot of. But realize that you're spending more money up front to achieve savings in the long run. So make sure you're going to use all of it, particularly if it has a limited life. Also, be sure you are in fact saving when you buy in bulk quantity. If the store has unit pricing, it will be easy to find out.

## ◆ 266  Stock up during seasonal sales.

Many seasonal sales are genuine sales. If you are good at planning ahead, you can save by taking advantage of a retailer's excess inventory.

## ◆ 267  When shopping, ignore those annoying announcements of special sales that will last only an hour or so.

It's slow-moving merchandise that no one wants. Still, you may want to saunter over to see the hordes of people trying to take advantage of the "bargain."

## ◆ 268  Don't be taken in by promotions.

For example, don't subscribe to a magazine because they'll give you a free clock radio or a videotape of athletes doing stupid things. If you want a clock radio, buy a clock radio, not a magazine.

## ◆ 269  Return purchases that are unsatisfactory.

Don't be a wimp. If you buy something that doesn't meet your expectations, return it. Remember, it's your hard-earned money, and when you buy something, you have every right to receive complete satisfaction with the product. Also, the stores with which you do business want *you* to be happy. Believe me, the 1990s is going to be a tough decade for every retail business, so you'll find them more willing than ever to make sure you're a satisfied customer.

### ♦ 270  Return purchases that are unneeded.

If you buy something and later find you don't need the item you bought, return it. Don't rationalize "Well, maybe I'll end up needing this item someday." Instead, take it back next time you go to the store. I recently spent $13 on a gallon of liquid that removes mildew. When I showed it to my wife, she said she could mix up a home potion that would do the same job. I returned it. Make better use of your money; don't hold on to something that you may need a long time hence or that you may never need.

### ♦ 271  Buy furniture from a local discounter.

Furniture discounters are sprouting up all over the country, and you can save a substantial amount by patronizing them. They usually offer a wide selection of home furnishings, but if you don't find what you want at a particular showroom, visit another one.

### ♦ 272  Buy furniture by mail.

Several companies offer brand-name furniture through the mail. These companies usually represent several leading furniture manufacturers, and they provide a wide variety of choices at considerably lower prices than you could find at a low-price furniture store. The downside is that you'll have to wait, often several months, before the furniture is delivered. But the wait may well be worth the often substantial savings of buying through these companies.

### ♦ 273  Buy furniture directly from the manufacturer.

If you're willing to wait several months, you could save a bundle on furniture by buying directly from the manufacturer. Many of them will be more than happy to provide you with a catalog and ordering information.

### ♦ 274  Buy knockdown furniture.

It used to be that the three worst words in the English language were "some assembly required." While this is still true of many products, particularly children's toys, the knockdown furniture business has come a long way. Don't be intimidated by furniture that requires some assembly. You can get high-quality furniture pieces that you can assemble easily and not tell from the finished piece that it was assembled by you. The savings of knockdown furniture are usually considerable.

## ◆ 275 Buy unfinished furniture.

You don't need to be a Michelangelo to do a satisfactory job on furniture finishing. With the materials available, you'll surprise yourself at your skill. If you still are not convinced, why not first try finishing a piece for the children's room? Even if you don't do a very good job, it won't matter—the kids will destroy it anyway.

## ◆ 276 Spray upholstered furniture with fabric protector.

Don't risk ruining a nice piece of furniture because of an accidental spill. Invest in a couple of cans of spray-on fabric protector and avert disaster.

## ◆ 277 Reupholster or refinish furniture rather than discard it.

What a shame to discard furniture that can be so easily refurbished. Before you discard some furniture, find out how much it would cost to put it in like-new condition, and compare that with the cost of replacing it.

## ◆ 278 Don't buy durable goods that will last longer than you need them.

A swing set is a good example of this. Some of them are guaranteed for twenty years, and by the looks of these formidable structures they will last at least that. But ask yourself: Do you plan to have children who will still make use of the swing set twenty years from now? Therefore, don't buy the Rolls-Royce of durable goods when the Chevrolet will do.

### ◆ 279   Buy seasonal appliances off-season.

In other words, buy air conditioners in the fall and buy heaters in the spring. If you can anticipate your needs ahead of time, rather than waiting for the thermometer to reach a hundred before going out to buy an air conditioner, you can save money. This strategy is similar to investing in stocks: Buy stocks when no one else is buying them. Conversely, like stocks, if you ever want to sell the air conditioner or heater, you would, of course, sell it when everyone else wants it.

### ◆ 280   Don't buy a home computer unless you are sure you're going to make good use of it.

A computer is a big investment, so be realistic in your assessment of how much use you will get out of it. Far too many computers are bought with the best of intentions, only to end up collecting dust. True, they can do a lot of things, and they can be entertaining as well, but are you really going to make sufficient use of a personal computer to justify its cost?

### ◆ 281   Don't buy appliance service contracts.

While they may seem inexpensive, particularly in relation to the amount you are already shelling out for the appliance, most experts agree they're a waste of money. Better to decline and take your chances. Don't be surprised if you get a sales pitch on this, because the salesperson probably gets a hefty commission if he or she sells the contract.

### ◆ 282   Don't buy computer software unless you know you're going to use it.

Some experts have suggested that over 90 percent of purchased computer software goes unused: a waste of money. Don't get lured into buying a piece of software unless you know you're going to make good use of it. If you have unused software sitting around the house, you might try to sell it to one of your computer-nut friends.

### ◆ 283 Buy toothpaste by the tube.

While the other dispensers may be convenient, you don't seem to get much toothpaste for the money. Sometimes old-fashioned is better, and you can usually be sure that "new and improved" means that the product might be improved and the new price is higher.

### ◆ 284 A used-up toothpaste tube isn't necessarily used up.

No matter how much you squeeze a toothpaste tube, chances are there still is some paste left. So when you're certain you've squeezed the last drop, cut open the tube and I'll bet you'll be able to brush once more.

### ◆ 285 Buy artificial plants rather than live ones.

Live plants are wonderful, but they eat. And anything that eats costs money. Besides, they also die. The science of artificial plant manufacturing has come a long way in recent years. Many look great, so you may want to consider buying some.

### ◆ 286 Buy assorted greeting cards in quantity rather than individually.

If you buy greeting cards in bulk, you will not only save money as opposed to paying outrageous prices charged for individual greeting cards, you'll also save innumerable $5 automobile trips to the card shop to buy a $1 card.

### ◆ 287 Next time you need sunglasses, cheaper is probably better.

If you think that expensive sunglasses offer better eye protection, you're wrong. Ophthalmologists generally agree that all you need are plastic lenses that offer "UV" protection. Perfectly adequate eye protection sunglasses should cost no more than $10. If you pay more, you're only indulging your vanity.

### ◆ 288 Subscribe to magazines rather than buying them at newsstands.

If you're a regular reader of a magazine, you'll save a lot of money by subscribing rather than buying it at the newsstand.

On the other hand, if you're thinking of subscribing to a magazine, first buy a couple of issues at the newsstand to make sure you're sufficiently interested to subscribe.

◆ **289** **Ask friends who subscribe to give you the magazine and book review sections from major Sunday newspapers.**

A lot of people buy the Sunday newspaper and end up reading only a few sections. If this describes you, ask friends who devour Sunday newspapers to give you the sections that most interest you after they are finished with them. If you're both Sunday newspaper junkies, you could alternate buying the paper, in which case you would agree to turn over the entire paper at a certain time.

◆ **290** **Never buy anything that has any of the following words on its packaging or advertising: gourmet, exclusive, limited edition, connoisseur, select, limited time offer.**

The only thing special about these items is that they are especially expensive.

◆ **291** **Freeze candles before using them.**

Your enchanted evening will last a lot longer.

◆ **292** **Cut off the handles of discarded brooms and mops.**

Broom handles without the broom attached and mop handles without mops attached make great gardening stakes.

◆ **293** **If you are buying an area rug, check the remnants section of the carpet store.**

Before sinking your money into an area rug taken right off the roll at full price, check to see if there are some remnants at the store that can satisfy your carpeting and cost-cutting requirements. Better yet, visit the remnants section of several carpet stores. I bet you'll find what you need.

## ♦ 294   Buy generic or unfamiliar-name cosmetics.

Why pay for the huge amount of advertising expense that goes into promoting brand-name cosmetics? Buy generic brands or brands you never heard of for considerably less. Don't accept the argument that you have to use twice as much of the generic product to accomplish what you can get from the name brand. Find out for yourself. Even if that is the case, chances are the unfamiliar branded product costs a third as much, so you're still ahead of the game financially. That's what counts.

## ♦ 295   Buy queen-size top sheets for king-size beds.

You need a king's ransom to be able to afford king-size sheets. Check the price difference between queen-size and king-size sheets. You'll be delighted to know that a queen-size top sheet usually fits your king-size bed.

## ♦ 296   Lengthen the time between visits to the beauty or barber shop.

I'm not suggesting you need to look like Rapunzel, but if you're looking for ways to cut your expenses, have your hair cut and styled less often. Some people get into the habit of visiting the local tonsorial parlor too frequently. After all, it's nice to have your plumage spruced, but it's an expense that can be reduced by making those visits less frequently.

## ♦ 297   Find a less expensive beauty salon or barber shop.

Being pampered costs money. If you're willing to put up with a little less, you'll be able to pamper your purse a little more.

## ♦ 298   Get coiffed at a beauty or barber school.

If your town has a beautician or barber school, inquire about their cut-rate services. This is not for everyone, but some people swear by them. Not only are you saving money, you're helping an aspiring barber or beautician.

## ◆ 299  Don't send packages via first-class mail.

Unless it is urgent, use parcel post rather than first-class or priority mail to send packages.

## ◆ 300  Save good cartons for storage.

You know good from bad. Save the good. They may come in handy for storage. (A sturdy carton can protect your storage possessions from alien forces such as dust and dirt.) Also, they can help you organize your storage so it takes up less space, meaning there is less likelihood you'll lose something. But don't start to store boxes, because they can become a storage problem themselves.

## ◆ 301  Collect the loose change lying around the house.

My two preschoolers are empowered to take any change that's lying around the house as long as they place it in their piggy banks. These resourceful munchkins may find enough loose change to pay for their college! (The parents certainly hope so.) Don't let loose change just accumulate. Wrap it and deposit it somewhere so it can earn interest.

## ◆ 302  Write your member of Congress for a free calendar.

Why pay for a calendar when you can get it free simply by writing your U.S. congressman or senator? You don't have to promise you'll vote for them to get your calendar, but they'll appreciate it if you would.

## ◆ 303  Contact the Consumer Information Center for useful government publications.

U.S. government publications are sadly underutilized national treasures. Write the Consumer Information Center, Pueblo, CO 81009, and ask for the *Consumer's Resource Handbook*, which has over two thousand sources to help with consumer problems. The price of this booklet is also right: It's free.

◆ **304** **If you buy something on sale, put the savings in the bank.**

If you really want to prove that you actually save money when buying something on sale, put the amount of money you "saved" in a savings or investment account.

◆ **305** **Quit feeling like you have to keep up with your friends' or neighbors' profligate spending habits.**

One of the surest ways to bankrupt yourself is to try to keep up with the Joneses. Everyone has neighbors or friends who live beyond their means and love to brag about it. They're experts at making you feel like some poor slob. Of course you envy them a little—we would all like to have more—but take heart. You have something far more valuable than they have: good sense. Rather than envied, they should be pitied. Free spending and conspicuous consumption are no-no's, especially in the 1990s.

# IV

# BIG-TICKET ITEMS

# 10

# Health Care

The already high and steadily rising costs of health care: There is much we can do to control them, and it begins with taking better care of ourselves. Also, we should be better health care consumers. While it may be true that when it comes to your good health, cost is no object, wise shopping for health care insurance, medical and dental services, and medicinal products can result in real savings while maintaining the excellent health care you want for yourself and your loved ones.

## ◆ 306 Always, always, always maintain good health insurance coverage.

The quickest way to lose what you have accumulated over your lifetime as well as, perhaps, a large chunk of your future income is to suffer an uninsured illness. Do whatever is necessary to maintain adequate health insurance coverage for you and every family member. Be particularly careful about your elderly parents: Do they have Medicare gap insurance? Also, do your adult children have health insurance coverage through their place of employment or, if they are "between jobs," have they purchased a temporary health insurance policy?

## ◆ 307 Don't get sick.

Preventive medicine is the cheapest medicine. Learn how to stay healthy, then spend all of the money you save on yourself.

### ♦ 308 Don't wait until you get too sick to see a doctor.

Most of us are crazy when it comes to our own health. If our car sputters, we immediately take it to a mechanic. If our dog coughs, it's off to the vet ASAP. But if we have an apparent health problem, do we go to our doctor? All too often the answer is "no," until the problem worsens. The worse the health problem, the more expensive it is going to be to you, no matter how comprehensive your health coverage. So don't postpone seeing your doctor if one of you starts to sputter or cough.

### ♦ 309 Get a physical examination at regular intervals.

Preventive medicine is still about the best thing we've got going for us to maintain good health and control health care costs. Follow your doctor's suggestion to get a periodic physical examination. Chances are the poking and stabbing will show you to be in good shape. If there is a problem, it's far better (and cheaper) to know sooner rather than later.

### ♦ 310 Quit smoking.

Smoking is hazardous to your financial health. The habit can easily cost over $1,000 per year, not to mention what it does to your health insurance and life insurance premiums, and dental bills.

### ♦ 311 Try to lose weight on your own.

Consult with a doctor, buy a couple of diet books, and really try to lose weight on your own before going to an expensive weight-loss clinic. The one thing that's certain about a weight-loss clinic is that they'll certainly put your wallet on a diet.

### ♦ 312 Watch your weight.

Excess weight and/or the ordeal of constantly gaining and losing weight is likely to cause health problems sooner or later. As difficult as it is, if you can attain and maintain a reasonable weight, you will stand a better chance of avoiding a number of weight-related health problems and the resulting high out-of-pocket costs.

### ♦ 313 Don't drink excessively or spend excessively to drink.

You can cut your liquor bills considerably by sticking to wine and beer and keeping it local. Many fine products are made in America. You don't need to spend a fortune on German beer and French wine.

### ♦ 314 Brush and floss your teeth regularly.

This suggestion can save you a lot of pain, both physical and financial. Many of the calamities that befall our teeth and gums are avoidable with regular brushing and flossing. Just remember the tacky sign that you may have seen staring you in the face as you sat in your dental chair: "You don't have to brush and floss all of your teeth, just the ones you want to keep."

### ♦ 315 Have your children's teeth coated.

Take advantage of some of the great advances in dental care that have been made in recent years. One is teeth coating for children, which will prevent cavities from occurring later. Inquire of your own dentist or your children's dentist about the procedure. Hopefully your children will be able to say, as the old ad goes, "Look, Ma, no cavities." You'll both benefit. Your kids will have no cavities in their teeth, and you'll have no cavity in your pocketbook through which money flows to your kids' dentist.

### ♦ 316 Be sure to keep your immunizations up-to-date.

Make sure you and all family members stay immunized. Unfortunately, some locales are experiencing outbreaks of easily preventable diseases. These diseases would never have gotten a foothold had everyone kept their immunizations up-to-date.

◆ **317** Take advantage of publicly sponsored vaccinations.

Inquire of the local health department about free or reduced-cost vaccinations and immunizations. Take advantage of them when available.

◆ **318** Don't hesitate to rely on public health nurses for assistance when needed.

If you or a loved one requires home care, contact your local health dept or Visiting Nurse Association (VNA) to find out what they offer and how you can qualify. You'll be surprised at the number of health programs available to people who need them despite all the highly publicized cutbacks in these programs. Don't give up.

◆ **319** Use sunblock.

Just as overspending is "out" in the 1990s, so are deep suntans. Bronzed bodies may look good, but an increasing medical consensus believes that deep suntans could cost you dearly—both physically and financially—in later life.

◆ **320** Investigate alternative health care plans offered by your employer.

If you are fortunate enough to work for a company that offers a choice of health care plans, don't just assume that the one you have is the best. Review alternatives. Some plans may cost you less while meeting the health care needs of you and your family.

◆ **321** Take advantage of the COBRA regulations if you lose your job or are divorcing.

It sounds like a snake, but it is actually an important law that requires employers to continue health insurance coverage for specified periods for employees who leave their jobs or employee-spouses who are divorcing. While the employee or spouse has to pay for the coverage, this is far better than losing essential health insurance coverage.

## ◆ 322  Get a second opinion.

It is usually wise to get a second opinion before undertaking any significant, and hence expensive, medical procedure. Your health insurance carrier may pay for the second opinion, which shows how much the insurer values the money-saving potential of second opinions.

## ◆ 323  Examine your hospital and doctor bills.

Even if your insurer is picking up the tab, be sure to scrutinize hospital and doctor bills. If you find any discrepancies, be sure to holler. We all need to pitch in if we have any hope of controlling the skyrocketing costs of health care.

## ◆ 324  Investigate health and dental services available at a medical or dental school at no or reduced cost.

If you live near a university medical or dental school, you may be able to take advantage of health and dental services offered by the school as part of its students' training. The price is right, since the charges, if any, are nominal. Rest assured that the student examining or treating you is fully supervised and very diligent.

## ◆ 325  Don't use the emergency room for routine health care.

Establish a relationship with a doctor or medical group so you will have somewhere to turn if and when health care problems arise. Far too many people end up using the emergency room for nonurgent medical purposes, which is both wasteful and costly. The emergency room will understandably charge an arm and a leg for people whose health care needs are not urgent.

## ◆ 326  Take your own essentials to the hospital.

Save money by bringing some of your own essentials, such as tissues and toothpaste, to the hospital. Of course, the hospital would be happy to provide you with them, but at a cost that will leave you gasping for breath.

## ◆ 327 Buy generic drugs.

Generic drugs save you money. In many instances they are identical to those with brand names. Your physician or pharmacist will be glad to help you decide when to select the generic. If you want to save even more money, buy generics through the mail.

## ◆ 328 Don't get cosmetic surgery.

Unless you're really up for improving your appearance and willing to pay through the nose for it, avoid getting cosmetic surgery for vanity purposes. It probably won't be covered by your health insurance, and most cosmetic surgery is no longer includable as a deductible medical expense for income-tax purposes.

## ◆ 329 Want to change your appearance and save on income taxes?

Get a sex-change operation. It will probably count as an allowable medical expense. On the other hand, a face-lift probably will not qualify. Does this seem incongruous? A sex-change operation performed on a doctor's orders (better get it in writing) will probably not be challenged. On the other hand, the tax rules have been changed with respect to cosmetic surgery: Unnecessary cosmetic surgery no longer qualifies as a deductible medical expense. The lesson here is that if you're having an elective medical procedure, don't automatically assume that the cost will qualify as a medical expense for income-tax purposes.

## ◆ 330 Wear eyeglasses instead of contacts.

Even fairly expensive eyeglasses with scratchproof, ultraviolet-resistant lenses will cost you less over the long run than the hundreds of little vials of solutions you'll need to clean your contact lenses. Besides, you probably won't tear or lose your eyeglasses.

## ◆ 331 Seek alternatives to health clubs.

Unless you go to a health club to socialize, it can be a very expensive way to exercise. Cut your exercise costs by purchasing your own equipment: Used equipment is a steal; use a public pool or gym; go for a run in the park; or join the local YMCA or JCC at a nominal cost.

## ◆ 332 Don't join a health club thinking you can get a medical or business deduction.

Some people justify their joining a health club by thinking they can either get a business-expense deduction or a medical-expense deduction. After all, your improved physical condition will enhance your health and make you a more effective employee. Some of the health clubs, in their zeal to get you to sign up, even imply that this is possible. But it isn't under most circumstances.

## ◆ 333 Automobile expenses to attend Alcoholics Anonymous meetings can qualify as medical expenses.

The IRS has deemed travel to Alcoholics Anonymous, Narcotics Anonymous, and other such self-help organizations as qualifying for a medical-expense deduction. So while you strive to improve your own physical and mental health, you may improve your financial health as well.

## ◆ 334 Don't forget parking fees and tolls associated with medical travel.

Far too many people simply use the standard mileage rate when they use their car for medical purposes. But tolls and parking can be added to the tab. Also, if you're smart enough to take the bus or train to meet your medical appointments, don't forget to include the fares as part of your total medical expenses for tax purposes.

## ◆ 335 If drugs or alcohol is becoming a problem, seek help now.

Drug and alcohol problems are devastating to the addicted, to their families, and to society as a whole. If you find that you or a loved one is experiencing these problems, seek help now; don't delay. The sooner you resolve your addiction, the sooner you'll be able to return to an emotionally, physically, and financially productive life.

### ◆ 336 Keep track of auto mileage associated with medical care.

Any medical care–associated travel you have to make—seeing doctors, dentists, etc.—is deductible as a medical expense subject to the 7.5 percent of AGI (adjusted gross income) limitation. If you use your car, either deduct the actual cost of gas and oil, or take a simpler approach by using the standard mileage rate.

### ◆ 337 Keep records of nonreimbursed medical expenses.

It seems that the only way you can figure out whether your medical expenses will exceed the 7.5 percent of AGI threshold is to keep all nonreimbursed medical expenses, including payments you make for your children and for any other dependents for whom you provide more than half of the total support for the year. This may seem like an onerous task, but what better investment of your time if you can end up saving on taxes?

### ◆ 338 Accelerate the payment of needed medical expenses and procedures by the end of the year if you are or will be over the 7.5 percent of AGI threshold.

Around the time you begin your Christmas shopping, it's time to tote up your medical expenses to see how you stand. If you expect to exceed the 7.5 percent threshold, bring all your bills up-to-date to the extent possible.

### ◆ 339 When determining if you exceed the 7.5 percent threshold for deductible medical expenses, be sure to include all payments.

Many people, when adding up total expenses for the year, forget to include some of the medical costs they paid that can qualify for tax purposes. Such items include expenses incurred by any dependents (children or parents) for whom you provide more than half of the total support for the year. Also, be sure to add in all prescription drugs. When you add up all these expenses, you may be pleasantly surprised to find that you do exceed the 7.5 percent AGI threshold, and you can take pleasure in a newfound tax deduction.

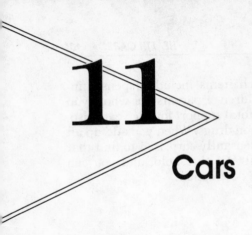

# Cars

Most people spend far more to own and maintain their cars than they can comfortably afford. It used to be that people spent the equivalent of about two months' salary on a car, and if they didn't pay cash for it, they financed it over eighteen months at most. Now people spend a fortune for a car, finance it over an eternity, and then turn around and buy another car within a few years. No wonder so many people can't afford to save for the important things in life, such as a home, a college education for their kids, and a comfortable retirement.

I hate cars. I'm proud to drive around in an old clunker. A few years ago a neighbor put the following note on my windshield: "Your car violates this neighborhood's standards of good taste." I took that as a compliment, because I knew that if I had fallen into the trap of always wanting a late-model car, I couldn't have afforded to live in that neighborhood. There are so many ways to reduce the wasteful costs of car ownership. Many are described below.

## ◆ 340   Keep your cars longer.

There's no reason why you can't keep a car for seven to ten years or even longer. People who trade their cars in every three, four, or five years are simply throwing money away. Sure, a late-model car feels good, and you probably think people are impressed by it. But is it worth the cost?

### ◆ 341 Leave the car at home and use public transportation.

You can save a bundle by taking public transportation rather than driving. It is not a sign of poverty to use public transportation; it's a sign of good sense.

### ◆ 342 Use a bike rather than a car.

Why not use a bike rather than a car for short trips? Driving short distances is just plain wasteful.

### ◆ 343 If you're a city dweller, rent rather than own a car.

If you live in a major city, owning a car borders on the financially ridiculous. Parking is expensive, insurance is expensive, and your car will really suffer with stop-and-go city driving. Unless you need to use a car regularly, renting rather than owning a car makes more financial sense. This is particularly true if you tend to use your car on weekends only. Weekend rental rates are discounted.

### ◆ 344 Sell your second (or third) car.

Do you really need so many cars? Do you remember the days when families got along perfectly well with one, or at most two cars? I know people who have as many as five cars but only two drivers in the family! What's going on?

### ◆ 345 Buy a good used car rather than an expensive new car.

The quickest way to lose $2,000 is to drive a new car off the dealer's lot. So many people are obsessed with frequently trading in their cars, there are many excellent used cars that go begging. If you get into the habit of buying used cars, you'll save literally tens of thousands of dollars over your lifetime.

◆ **346**   **Don't buy vanity plates.**

Why pay extra to indulge your ego with a personalized license plate? If you must have your initials on your car, why don't you just paint them on the trunk lid in foot-high letters?

◆ **347**   **Pay cash for your car.**

Interest on personal car loans is no longer deductible—so pay cash and save yourself money.

◆ **348**   **Do your homework before purchasing a car.**

The only way to assure a good deal from a car salesman is to march into the showroom heavily armed with facts and figures. You should know exactly which car you want to purchase, including the options you want, and you should know *exactly* what the dealer has paid for the particular car you want to buy. Let's face it: It's you against the dealer, and if you don't have the right information, you're at a big disadvantage.

◆ **349**   **Shop for the best auto loan deals.**

The best auto loans probably won't be at the dealership. Check your credit union and seek a better deal.

◆ **350**   **Finance cars over three years or less.**

Some people never manage to get out from under a car loan. If you can't afford to finance a car over two or three years, you can't afford that car.

◆ **351**   **Buy cars at the end of the month.**

You may find that your friendly car dealer is more anxious to deal with you at the end of the month, when quotas must be met. One way to test this out is to start to deal in earnest within a few days of the end of the month, and then, if you think you've got a reasonably good deal, tell the salesperson you want to "think it over" for a few days and you'll get back around the first or second of the following month. Never feel guilty about manipulating auto dealers, because you can be assured they will manipulate you at any and every opportunity.

### ◆ 352 Buy cars at the end of the model year.

Since I hope you will keep your car forever, it really doesn't matter when during the model year you purchase it. That being the case, cars are cheaper at the end of the model year, as car dealers need to clear out their inventories and the manufacturers provide additional financial incentives to the dealers to move the remaining inventory. Whatever time of the year you buy, however, make sure you're well informed about dealer costs and manufacturer's incentives, and negotiate like a pro. You might even want to wait until the beginning of the next model year, because most dealers will have some of last year's models sitting on the lot, and the only thing they are attracting is dust.

### ◆ 353 Shop around when buying a car.

An automobile is probably your second biggest expense. Indeed, for far too many people, it is their biggest expense. Why, therefore, rely on the first dealer's offer when making a purchase? Shop around and let each and every dealer know that you are shopping around. Otherwise you are going to be taken for a ride in more ways than one.

### ◆ 354 Avoid cars that are more costly to insure.

Insurance companies are no dummies. They maintain extensive records on the claims they have to pay out by car model. Don't waste money buying a car that, for whatever reasons— perhaps it has twenty-five cylinders and three hundred valves and can exceed the speed of sound—incurs higher premiums than more ordinary vehicles.

### ◆ 355 Don't get frivolous options on your car.

A "loaded" car means two things. First, it means that it is loaded with all of the available options. Second, it means that it is going to be loaded with problems in the future as these options start to fall apart. When you next buy a car, evaluate carefully how much you need each option. Some of them, such as a sunroof, cost a lot of money and serve no apparent purpose. Not only does a loaded car end up costing several thousand dollars more up front, but you will also pay dearly in the future keeping these options functioning.

♦ **356** **If you want to buy the dealer's "extras" when you buy a new car, pay to have your head examined instead.**

Such extras are commonly called "packs." They're as close to worthless as anything you could ever buy. "Packs" include items such as undercoat, overcoat, racing stripes, and, of course, the infamous fabric protector. If the dealer asks if you would like to add one of these packages to your gleaming new car, just laugh. If he or she then informs you that they already have been added to the car, thank them kindly and then tell them you're not going to pay for them.

♦ **357** **Don't buy extended service contracts.**

Your automobile dealer will love to sell you an extended service contract—one that covers you beyond the manufacturer's warranty. While they may sound like a bargain, you'll probably end up paying more for the service contract than you will for repairs that are covered by the contract. (If this wasn't true, they wouldn't be selling the contract to you.) The only exception: If you're such an awful driver that your car is constantly in the shop, you might benefit from an extended service contract, but read the fine print. They probably have got some exclusions that apply to your type of driving. A better alternative would be to start driving sensibly, because an extended service contract won't stop your bad driving habits from driving you to the poorhouse.

♦ **358** **Consider using an automobile broker to buy a car.**

Automobile brokers can deliver the car of your choice for a slight premium over dealer cost. They are an alternative worth considering, although you will want to check them out before doing business with them. Be particularly careful if you plan to order an imported car through a broker. You will need to make sure that the car is manufactured to meet U.S. emission standards.

### ◆ 359 Don't lease a car.

I have two big problems with car leasing. First, leasing is always more expensive than buying a car with borrowed money. True, in some cases, you will find a leasing deal that comes close to the cost of purchasing a particular vehicle outright, but even these deals are generally slightly more expensive. Second, even if leasing does become a more cost-effective method of ownership, it still motivates people to trade their cars more frequently than they should. Leasing deals tend to run three to five years when, in fact, you should be keeping your car seven to ten years.

### ◆ 360 Consider buying a "demonstration" car with a new-car guarantee.

You may be able to get a good bargain with a dealer who sells "demonstrators," cars with low mileage that the dealer has used for a variety of purposes, including test rides. The dealer will typically offer a reasonably good discount on the car along with a new-car guarantee. You also may want to consider buying a low-mileage vehicle from a rental agency.

### ◆ 361 Buy used cars only from a responsible dealer, preferably someone with whom you have already done business.

While it is usually preferable to buy a used car rather than to spend a fortune on a new vehicle, you must be particularly careful when buying an automobile on the "secondary market." Often it's better to buy your car from a responsible dealer—who has a good reputation in the community and who will stand by the vehicle he or she has sold you—even if lower prices are available elsewhere.

## ◆ 362  Sell your old car yourself.

Chances are that you can sell your old car for quite a bit more money than the dealer will give you as a trade-in on a new car. Sure, it takes a little effort, but time is well spent if you can make a little extra money to put toward your next chariot. (If you keep your car as long as I do, only the junk dealer will buy it.)

## ◆ 363  Slow down.

Driving at the speed limit not only improves your gas mileage but also avoids the expense (and annoyance) of those nasty moving violations.

## ◆ 364  Drive carefully.

As trite as it may sound, one of the best ways to reduce the horrendous costs of driving a car is to drive carefully. Avoiding accidents (whether they're your fault or not), traffic violations, and driving erratically will save money. Your insurance costs will be lower, your car maintenance costs will be lower, you won't be confronted with paying deductibles for accidents, and you'll avoid supporting the local municipal government with traffic fines. If you have a long period of accident-free driving and have a first accident, you may still avoid an increase in rates if your insurer forgives a first offense to good long-term customers.

## ◆ 365  Avoid quick starts and stops, especially in heavy traffic.

Stop-and-go driving burns up brakes, gasoline, oil, and tires.

## ◆ 366  Brake slowly.

If you brake sensibly rather than suddenly, you will save hundreds of dollars on brake jobs over the life of your car. Also, the discipline of anticipating your stops and thus not jamming on your brakes should help you avoid accidents as well.

# ◆ 367  Keep your car windows closed.

You used to sacrifice gas mileage when you closed car windows and turned on the air conditioner. This is no longer the case: Cars have been designed to run most efficiently with the windows closed, even with the air conditioning on. In other words, you now sacrifice gas mileage by keeping your windows open.

# ◆ 368  Store change in your car for parking meters.

Most cities and towns are desperate to raise money, so you are likely to encounter an increasing number of parking meters. Be sure to keep plenty of change stashed away in the car—out of plain view—so you'll be able to feed these voracious meters. At the rate things are going in my town, pretty soon they'll charge 25 cents for each minute of parking. If you've got sufficient change in the car, you'll resist the temptation to take a chance. Remember, you can feed a lot of meters for the price of one $5, $10, or $20 parking violation.

# ◆ 369  Check for a parking meter that still has time left on it.

Whenever you have to park in a lot or on a street with meters, look around for a meter with some time left on it. What a wonderful discovery!

# ◆ 370  Avoid toll roads if you can take an alternate route that won't waste gasoline and time.

Sometimes you can do just as well driving parallel to a turnpike as you can by driving on it, particularly if traffic on the toll road tends to be congested. Also, you might be able to save a little money by planning to enter a turnpike a couple of exits closer to your destination. Maybe I'm crazy, but I always find it challenging to find alternate routes to beat the toll-takers out of a couple of quarters. Note to people who fly into LaGuardia Airport in New York City: If you must take a cab to or from Manhattan (the Carey bus or a city bus/subway are a lot cheaper), tell the driver to take you over the Fifty-ninth Street Bridge. This bridge has no toll, while both the Triborough Bridge and the Midtown Tunnel have hefty tolls. The Fifty-ninth Street Bridge is the most direct route as well, and except for rush hour, is probably the quickest way to get to Manhattan from LaGuardia.

### ◆ 371 Be sure your power train is adequate to handle your trailer, boat, etc.

Don't try to haul more than your car can handle, especially in hilly areas.

### ◆ 372 Clean up your car to reduce its weight.

Do you use your backseat and trunk as a rolling warehouse? If so, clean it out. It will reduce the weight of the car and therefore the cost of driving it.

### ◆ 373 Combine various errands into one trip.

Organize your life so you can use your car more efficiently. Combine several errands into one trip. If you find yourself taking the car out several times a week just to do one thing, you can be certain you're wasting hard-earned money. A little advance planning will reduce the wear and tear on your car.

### ◆ 374 Put last year's telephone directory in the trunk of your car.

How many times have you driven around and around trying to find a store or home when you have forgotten or misplaced its address? Suppose you had a phone book handy. You could save time and gasoline by pulling over, getting the directory out, and letting your fingers do some navigating.

### ◆ 375 Learn to perform routine car maintenance yourself.

Have you noticed the labor charges for car maintenance and repairs lately? While not quite up there with neurosurgeons' fees, they're getting there. You can perform more routine maintenance tasks on your car than you think.

### ◆ 376  Pump your own gas.

Gas is too expensive to begin with, so why pay extra to have someone pump the liquid gold into your chariot?

### ◆ 377  Use regular unleaded fuel.

Chances are, unless your car has a jet engine, you can get by perfectly well with regular unleaded fuel. The higher-octane stuff is usually a lot more expensive. So avoid it unless your engine clearly needs it. By the way, if your car engine needs to burn high-octane super-duper unleaded, you probably have more car than you really need.

### ◆ 378  Change oil regularly.

Since I hope you are going to drive your car several hundred thousand miles, one of the most important things to do is to change your oil and oil filter at least as regularly as the owner's manual specifies. Some people change it more regularly than the manufacturer recommends.

### ◆ 379  Check your oil level regularly.

One of the problems with self-service gas stations is that we tend to neglect checking our oil regularly. If there's one way to ruin a sound automobile engine, it is the lack of sufficient oil. Check your oil every week or so, and do the same for your spouse's and kids' cars.

### ◆ 380  Monitor your car's supply of other "precious bodily fluids."

While the hood is up and you are checking the oil, also make sure you've got enough windshield wiper fluid. There's nothing worse than having some truck splash mud all over your windshield at the time when you discover your windshield washers are "running on empty." Also, check the levels on your automatic transmission fluid, power steering fluid, and radiator coolant. Finally, if winter is approaching, now's the time to make sure you have enough antifreeze. Okay, now you can close the hood.

### ◆ 381 Take care of your tires to save your car.

Rotate your tires periodically, and check the air in your tires regularly. Even if you pay to have these simple tasks done, it'll help you avoid replacing expensive tires prematurely.

### ◆ 382 Inspect your fan belts at least semiannually.

You can prevent a costly breakdown by periodically checking your fan belts for wear. Tip: Keep a spare set of fan belts in your trunk.

### ◆ 383 Wash and wax your car yourself instead of taking it to the car wash.

It really doesn't take that much time and effort to wash and wax your car periodically. The exercise is good for you, too, and since you'll be more fit, you'll live longer and be able to enjoy the money you saved by not enriching the local car wash.

### ◆ 384 Make sure the spare tire is fully inflated.

Flat tires happen so rarely that we never think to check to see if our spare tire is fully inflated—until it's too late. Don't risk the expensive service of your friendly tow truck. The per-mile rental charge on a 747 jetliner is cheaper than what they charge.

### ◆ 385 Buy your motor oil and other fluids at discount auto parts stores.

Why pay retail when you can get motor oil and other auto supplies at steep discounts? Do some people just like paying more?

### ◆ 386 Buy spare parts at the junkyard.

If you want to replace a fender or a door or some other auto part that does not involve the drive train, check out the junk dealer. He will probably have a perfectly good spare part at a fraction of the cost.

♦ **387** Find a good mechanic.

Auto dealers don't have a monopoly on good mechanics. As a matter of fact, some of them don't have any good mechanics. Like locating any other competent professional, word of mouth is often your best resource.

♦ **388** Don't have routine maintenance work done by the dealership.

Routine maintenance such as oil changes and tune-ups often are done more cheaply at a good service station or independent repair shop. Take the time to shop prices for this type of work.

♦ **389** Increase the deductible on your automobile insurance.

If you can afford to assume some of the financial risk yourself, increasing the deductible on your automobile insurance can reduce your premiums, often dramatically. While savings vary by company, increasing your deductible to $500 from $200 could reduce your collision premium by 15 to 30 percent.

♦ **390** Drop collision and/or comprehensive coverages on older cars.

If your car is worth $2,000 or less, (a) you have a marvelous older car with many years of good use still ahead of you and (b) you may want to drop your collision and/or comprehensive coverages, since these optional coverages might not be cost-effective.

♦ **391** Family cars can lower your insurance premiums.

Autos that are the favored targets of thieves are also more costly to insure. So do your family finances a favor and buy a frumpy car, one that is safe to drive and one that the average car thief would be embarrassed to steal.

◆ **392** **Insure all family cars with the same company.**

If you have more than one car, you can save about 15 to 20 percent on your fleet by insuring all the vehicles on a single policy with the same company.

◆ **393** **Put children on the parents' automobile insurance policy.**

You may get a premium discount if any of your family's younger drivers are attending a boarding school, college, or university at least a hundred miles from home. Keep them on your family's automobile insurance policy.

◆ **394** **Inquire about senior citizen auto insurance discounts.**

Drivers age fifty to fifty-five and older may qualify for discounts of up to 10 to 20 percent at some companies.

◆ **395** **Automatic seat belts and air bags may bring you an insurance discount.**

Most insurance companies offer discounts of 10 to 30 percent on the medical portion of the automobile insurance policy for owners of cars with automatic seat belts and/or air bags.

◆ **396** **Take a driver training course.**

Many auto insurance companies offer discounts for completing driver training or defensive driving courses. What's more, these courses may help you avert trouble on the road, which may be both a life- and a money-saver.

◆ **397** **Good standing in school can qualify you for a "good student" discount.**

Some insurance companies provide a discount for students who maintain a "B" average or better.

♦ **398** **Spend on antitheft devices and save on insurance.**

In some states, insurance carriers offer discounts on comprehensive coverage, usually 5 to 15 percent, for cars equipped with a hood lock and an alarm or disabling device that prevents the car from being started. In addition to the insurance saving, you also might avoid a costly car theft.

♦ **399** **If you drive less, your insurance may be less.**

Your insurance company may offer you a discount if you drive fewer than a stipulated number of miles per year.

♦ **400** **Don't duplicate the medical coverage provided by your health insurance policy when purchasing auto insurance.**

If you have an adequate health insurance policy, you may not need to take the medical payments or insured-motorist coverages in those states that do not require such coverage.

♦ **401** **Solo female drivers may qualify for a discount.**

Some auto insurance companies offer discounts for women age thirty to forty-nine, who are the only driver in a household.

♦ **402** **Inquire about occupational insurance discounts.**

Some insurance companies offer discounts if you are in a particular occupation. For example, farmers may receive discounts. On the other hand, if you drive a truck in the Bronx for a fireworks distributor, don't expect a discount.

♦ **403** **Keep your driver's license, car registration, and inspection stickers up-to-date.**

I just found this out the hard way. I was two days late renewing my registration, and the local constabulary presented me with a $100 fine. In these recessionary times your town is trying out "revenue enhancement" to make up for tax shortfalls. Don't help them out by procrastinating.

### ◆ 404 If you have an old car, investigate your state's antique-car statutes.

The Department of Motor Vehicles may offer reduced registration fees for your old clunker or your antique pride and joy.

### ◆ 405 Compare auto rental rates.

The only thing more in flux than auto rental rates is airfares. If you need to rent a car, I'll guarantee that you'll find vast differences in the offered rates. Take a few minutes to phone and find the best rates for your car rental needs. Rest assured, if you need to rent a car a week later, the rates will probably have changed, so you'll have to go through the same exercise.

### ◆ 406 Don't get optional coverage on auto rentals.

If you have an adequate automobile insurance policy, chances are you don't need the overpriced optional coverage the auto rental agencies try to convince you to purchase. If you are in doubt, check with your insurance agent. Why waste your money on unneeded coverage?

# 12

## College Students

This chapter is written for college students *and* their parents. You are in the same boat when it comes to the high cost of getting a college degree. While it has never been easy to pay for college, tuitions and fees rose dramatically over the past decade. The trend shows no signs of abating. Given college education's high cost, how do you bring it within your reach? First, by doing everything you can to secure the scholarships and financial aid your young scholar's entitled to. But that is just the beginning. Once settled into campus life, he or she should seek gainful part-time employment—it's typically plentiful in college towns. Also, holiday and summer jobs can help keep the family coffers from running dry. Finally, students should do their best to keep their living expenses under control. Not only is this helpful for the family, it also gives the student a head start on learning an essential real-life lesson: living beneath his or her means.

## ◆ 407 Investigate tuition payment options.

Meeting the cost of a college education is a struggle for all but the most affluent families. As a result, many schools have developed innovative tuition payment options that can ease the pinch. Be sure to investigate all the options offered by your child's school. Select the payment plan that best fits your own financial situation. If the school gives you the option of prepaying all four years of tuition, and you can afford to, do it. You will spare yourself the pain of future tuition hikes.

### ◆ 408 Avoid transferring assets to a child if you think you will qualify for financial aid.

While it is sometimes useful from a tax-planning standpoint for parents to transfer college-earmarked funds to a child's name, this strategy has backfired many times. For instance, when a student qualifies for financial aid, the student is required to use virtually all the money in his or her name—including any funds the parents gave their child—for college purposes. Had the transferred funds remained in the parents' name, the school would require them to use only half the money for tuition. So a word to the wise: Don't automatically assume that transferring funds to your children is a fail-safe financial strategy.

### ◆ 409 Give your college-age child an allowance that he or she can manage.

Your child may be either financially responsible or completely hopeless when it comes to managing money. If you are lucky enough to be the parent of a young John D. Rockefeller, there is probably no danger in giving a lump sum to him or her at the beginning of the semester. On the other hand, if your child hasn't yet learned financial self-discipline—and you're in the majority—he or she should be put on a monthly allowance. Better that your child calls you midway through the month to tell you that that month's dole is gone rather than to tell you that the whole semester's worth of funds has been squandered.

### ◆ 410 Ask your school to itemize the health care charges in your tuition bills separately.

Your parents are suffering enough to put you through college, so they'll appreciate knowing how much of the bill they pay goes toward medical costs. They can add that amount to the total family health bill to see if they can get a tax deduction.

### ◆ 411 Get good grades.

Good grades can accomplish a lot of things. First, they will keep your parents off your back; second, you may qualify for some merit-based scholarship or grant; third, many automobile insurance companies offer a "good student" discount if the student maintains a B average or better; and finally, good grades may help you land a job in this tough job market. I speak from experience about the value of good grades because, alas, I was one of those students who made it possible for my classmates to graduate in the top half of the class. I had a great time in college, but I was unable to reap the benefits that accrue to good students. While my classmates were graduating *cum laude*, I was graduating "thank you *laude*."

♦ **412** **Take a job at a college.**

Would you like to reduce your tuition costs to zero? If you work at a college or university, chances are your tuition will be waived. It's a good way to get a college education on the cheap—in some instances, you may even be able to receive tuition waivers for your children.

♦ **413** **Live in a dorm.**

Unless you plan to share an apartment with a horde of other people, your most economical housing bet is probably a dormitory. But beware: The desire to live off-campus often clouds a student's judgment. What initially appears to be cheaper than living in a dorm may end up costing a lot more.

♦ **414** **Buy used textbooks.**

Textbooks are unbelievably expensive. Pretty soon, textbooks are going to cost more than tuition. But you can reduce the cost of owning textbooks. If the particular text or texts you need haven't been newly updated, then there is no reason why you can't buy used editions. Before you buy the texts from the school bookstore, where the used textbooks have been given a stiff markup, try to buy them from a fellow student. If you eliminate the middleman—in this case the school bookstore—you will come out ahead.

♦ **415** **Get a part-time job.**

Colleges and college towns usually offer a plethora of part-time employment opportunities. As long as working doesn interfere with your studies, a part-time job is a good way to take some of the financial heat off your parents. You might even make some contacts that will help you find a real job after you graduate.

### ◆ 416 Don't pay dues to join an organization unless you plan to be active in it.

It's wonderful to provide some financial support to worthy student organizations through dues payments. Heaven knows, they always need funds, but don't write out a check to an organization unless you are going to benefit from it. Remember, it is real money you are paying out to this organization or that club. Be selective.

### ◆ 417 If you are on a meal plan, make maximum use of it.

I know that the cuisine served up in your school dining hall leaves something to be desired, but once you've paid for those meals, it's a terrible waste to skip them.

### ◆ 418 If you find you are missing meals on a regular basis, reduce your meal plan.

Even though it is a sin to miss meals that have already been bought, sometimes you may find that you are missing a lot of meals. For instance, some students are invariably unable to drag themselves out of bed in time for breakfast (woe be unto them when they start having to work for a living). If you find yourself in the meal-skipping rut, by all means select a reduced or limited meal plan.

### ◆ 419 Establish a cost-sharing arrangement with your roommate or roommates.

To avoid financial misunderstandings, you and your roommate or roommates should agree at the beginning of the school year on how to divvy up expenses such as phone service. Just like good fences supposedly make good neighbors, so a fair cost-sharing arrangement should make for a more harmonious relationship with your colleagues. You don't want to be worried about getting "stuck" by your roommate or roommates.

### ◆ 420 Make sure your personal possessions are insured.

Chances are that the valuables you have at school are covered under your parents' homeowner's or renter's insurance policy. Double-check this. If these items aren't covered, go to an insurance agent in your college's town and inquire about student policies. These policies are usually inexpensive, and it's probably worthwhile for you to purchase the coverage. Another thing to consider: If you have some particularly valuable items such as expensive jewelry, a stereo, or a fire-breathing computer system, verify that the policy does indeed cover your high-ticket items.

### ◆ 421 Do you really need a car at school?

Taking a car to school is a big expense. As difficult as it may be, try to evaluate objectively whether you really need a car at school. Sometimes having a car on-campus is a necessity, but in many instances students can get along very well without one.

### ◆ 422 Carpool home on vacations or weekends.

If you are driving home on a vacation or weekend, take a bunch of your comrades with you and ask them to kick in some gasoline money. If you're heading home without a car, hitch a ride with another student. It will be cheaper than alternative modes of transportation.

### ◆ 423 Start your job search early.

If you plan to work over Christmas vacation, spring breaks, or the summer, start your job search early. Well-paying and/or interesting jobs are in short supply, and the job market is competitive.

◆ **424** When you start your job, take advantage of moving expense deductions.

Tax regulations look favorably on people who have to move upon starting their first real job. It's far easier to qualify for moving-expense deductions if you're starting your first real job than it is if you're changing jobs, so chances are you'll qualify.

◆ **425** Take advantage of the tax break available to families who use U.S. savings bonds to pay for college.

You may be able to avail yourself of a nice tax break by buying U.S. savings bonds and using them to pay for your children's college education. There are rules aplenty, and the break is available only to families whose incomes don't exceed certain levels, so it's hard to predict whether you'll qualify. But it may be worth the risk. The worst that could happen is that you would have to pay taxes on the built-up interest on the bonds, which isn't so terrible. The important thing is that you will have accumulated a nice nest egg for the kids' education.

# V

# RELATIONSHIPS

# 13

# Courtship/
# Friendship

The choice is yours. You can either spend a fortune on your significant other or just plain friend, or you can take a more financially sensible approach. It's futile to try to buy genuine affection and friendship. Besides, in these days of personal financial restraint, free spending is more often a turnoff to prospective mates and friends. So why throw your money around? There is a more important person to whose welfare your extra money should be dedicated: you. The following thoughts will inject some reason into the financial aspects of both courtship and friendship.

### ◆ 426  Go dutch.

The convention that one party—usually the man—must shoulder the entire cost of a dinner, movie, or other entertainment has been jettisoned. It's fair to share, and the sooner you establish cost-splitting as a ground rule in a relationship, the better off you'll be—especially if you are the one who normally picks up the tab.

### ◆ 427  Date on the cheap.

Take advantage of the many free opportunities for amusement that make a good excuse for a date. The list is endless: biking, hiking, a visit to the park, free concerts, etc.

### ◆ 428  Don't go overboard on gift-giving to your sweetheart.

Ain't love grand—and ain't it expensive. Even though passion may be clouding your judgment, you must try to avoid spending more than you can afford on gifts for your significant other. You'll be glad to have saved some money if you ever decide to move in together. You can't sit or sleep on a sapphire ring or a gold watch.

## ◆ 429 Recognize that long-distance courtships are costly.

Before you get involved with some melancholy Ukrainian beauty, consider the costs that long-distance relationships invariably incur. Your phone bill will skyrocket, and you will find yourself earning many more frequent-flier miles than you had ever dreamed possible. And, if the relationship blossoms, one of you is going to have to move a long, long way. If you are already smitten, be sure to read the sections of this book concerning how to save money on telephone use, travel, and moving.

## ◆ 430 Celebrate Valentine's Day on February 15 or very late on February 14.

Once the end of Valentine's Day draws nigh, merchants are desperate to unload unsold gifts and candy. (Strike a deal with your florist over leftover Valentine's Day flower arrangements.) It's just as easy to show your love on February 15 as it is on February 14, and it could save you a hearty sum.

## ◆ 431 Fall in love with someone who is rich or at least affluent.

Let me tell you something: There is nothing romantic about falling in love with a poor person. It's just as easy to love a rich one. If you are looking for ways to ensure a secure financial future, "marrying well" is certainly a sensible way to reach that goal.

## ◆ 432 Don't fall for someone who has a lot of debt or other financial problems.

This happens a lot more often than you might realize—victims are too embarrassed to admit that they've been had. Say you fell for someone who is having debt problems. In a rush of love, you lend the person money to set him or her on an even financial keel. Suddenly the relationship sours. Kiss your money good-bye. (Many charlatans go from relationship to relationship in this manner.) Take my advice: Avoid falling for anyone who can't manage his or her personal finances.

### ♦ 433  Shop carefully for an engagement or wedding ring.

It's awfully easy to get taken when you are buying an engagement ring: Most of us don't buy diamond rings often enough to be informed bargainers. So educate yourself enough about diamonds so you can at least be an educated consumer. Also, visit only established dealers. Finally, don't spend more than you can comfortably afford.

### ♦ 434  Always use birth control.

There is nothing like an unintended pregnancy to sour a good relationship. Taking chances could be both financially and emotionally disturbing.

### ♦ 435  Never lend money to a friend.

The best way to destroy a good friendship is to lend money to or borrow money from a friend. If your friend can't borrow money from the usual sources, you can be assured that you are making a high-risk loan.

### ♦ 436  Don't spend too much money on things (such as clothes) that are intended to attract or keep a mate.

Don't go overboard on clothes, furniture, cars, or anything else you think will make you more attractive. Sure, we all like to put on the ritz, and sartorial finery has been a part of the mating ritual since Cleopatra snared Antony. But if your lover is attracted to you only because of your possessions, you have found someone unworthy of your affection.

# 14

## Marriage

Whoever said "Two can live as cheaply as one" must have lived alone. While many married couples enjoy two incomes, the costs of establishing a household and of raising children are onerous indeed. Whether you are betrothed or already married, the following exhortations will assist you in making the most of your—and your spouse's—money with a minimum of discord. Remember, however, that it's perfectly normal to argue periodically over family money matters. (Show me a married couple who has never had an argument over money and I'll show you a couple on the way to their own wedding reception.) Most couples do not disagree on their personal financial goals. It's the getting there that causes so many brouhahas. Perhaps it's because spenders tend to marry savers.

### ◆ 437 Have a less extravagant wedding.

Whether you or your parents are paying for your wedding, you can have a perfectly wonderful affair without breaking the bank. Extravagant weddings were a symbol of the free-spending 1970s and 1980s, but it is now chic to have a more intimate and less flashy to-do. Simplifying your wedding plans will save literally thousands of dollars, which can be put to much better use or, even better, saved.

♦ **438** **If you're having a traditional wedding, do your bridesmaids a favor by selecting bridesmaids' outfits that can be used for other formal occasions.**

Whoever is picking up the tab, it's wasteful to choose brides-maids' dresses or gowns that aren't suitable for other festive occasions.

♦ **439** **Engaged couples over age fifty-five may be able to wrangle a $250,000 capital-gains exclusion.**

If you and your spouse-to-be are both over age fifty-five and you both own homes and both homes have appreciated in value substantially, you could be entitled to a combined exclusion of $250,000 from the sale of your homes *if* both homes are sold prior to your marriage.

♦ **440** **Don't remarry before age sixty if you are a widow or widower who will be entitled to receive survivor's Social Security benefits.**

If you're entitled to begin receiving widow's benefits at age sixty, you will forfeit these valuable benefits if you marry before that age. That could be very costly.

♦ **441** **Work to keep your marriage intact.**

The single worst thing you can do to your financial health is to get divorced. Divorce takes a tremendous financial as well as emotional toll. Don't let your marriage lapse into divorce, which is all too common these days. Instead, work hard to keep your marriage afloat. It will be both emotionally and financially rewarding.

♦ **442** **Have fewer children.**

Raising a child costs about as much as a house, and a palatial one at that. From a financial standpoint, having fewer children makes a great deal of sense. Don't have more than you can comfortably afford.

◆ **443**  **Set aside one day each year to review your financial progress and plans for the future.**

Couples not only need to agree on what financial goals they want to accomplish in the long run, they must also decide how to go about reaching these goals. The best way to avoid periodic money squabbles is to sit down one day each year (in my family we have our powwow on April Fools' Day) to review your progress and discuss plans for the upcoming year. When you and your spouse have your "summit" you will also need to decide where to spend—and where to cut back—in the context of your overall financial planning.

◆ **444**  **Combine your investment accounts so that you pay only one account maintenance fee.**

Banks and brokerage firms are beginning to nickel-and-dime us to death. If you and your spouse maintain separate investment and savings accounts, each of which assesses a fee, consider combining accounts to save these annoying charges.

◆ **445**  **Buy only one of items you can share.**

Unless you are unusually persnickety, share a lot of everyday items with your spouse, such as shampoo, soap, and toothpaste.

◆ **446**  **If you must divorce, try mediation.**

Divorces are costly enough without running up huge legal bills. If both you and your spouse are amenable and are willing to settle the important matters without an adversarial proceeding, divorce mediation merits your consideration.

# 15

## Children

Children are wonderful. It's too bad they cost so much. While parents must resign themselves to the fact that their bundle of joy is also a bundle of childrearing expenses, there are many ways to reduce them. Unfortunately, far too many parents are caught up in the ridiculous feeling that they must bestow all things wonderful upon their little ones. This is not only expensive, it also sends the wrong message to the next generation. Follow the advice that's offered in this chapter, and both you and your child will be better off.

A tip: The magic words "We can't afford it" will help your children grow up to be financially responsible adults. These days, all too many children never hear these words.

### ◆ 447 Never take financial responsibility for anything that eats.

If you want to reduce your living expenses, never take financial responsibility for anything that eats. What qualifies? Children, spouses, pets, and plants. Of course, all of these bring joy to our lives, so eschewing them to save money may be a bit extreme, don't you think?

### ◆ 448 Don't let your children watch Saturday morning cartoons on network TV.

Sure, it's nice that the children are occupied on Saturday mornings—you can sleep in—but do you realize how many commercials they're being bombarded with? They will hit you up with requests for toys, cereals, and videos that were advertised on these programs; the aggregate value of these items would approach this year's federal deficit.

♦ **449** Form a baby-sitting cooperative.

Baby-sitters are a scarce and expensive commodity. It's getting to the point where the parents find that the biggest cost for a night on the town is the baby-sitter. That's why a lot of parents are forming baby-sitting cooperatives where they trade taking the chores of baby-sitting one another's brood. After all, it's already chaotic enough with a couple of your own kids around the house; taking care of a few more is no big deal.

♦ **450** Don't transfer a lot of money to your child's name.

A lot of well-meaning parents end up regretting this. First of all, although it can result in *some* tax savings, it usually doesn't save a lot. Unless you can afford to give your child tens of thousands of dollars, the tax reductions aren't going to be impressive. Second, what if you fall on tough times and need the money? Are you going to ask your nine-year-old for a loan? Third, what happens if, instead of going to college, your eighteen-year-old daughter joins a cult and falls in love with the cult leader? And, as luck would have it, the cult leader uses your daughter's money to buy another Rolls-Royce? These things have happened.

♦ **451** Live in (or move to) a town with a good school system rather than send your child to a private school.

Private schools are a very expensive proposition. If you're unhappy with your town's school system, consider relocating to a town with a superior public school system before making the substantial financial commitment to a private school education.

♦ **452** Remove expensive furniture and knick-knacks when children are around.

Sometimes I think the little terrors have radar. Put them in a room, and within five seconds they have the most expensive knickknack in hand, poised to launch it into orbit. Give a child a crayon and a coloring book and they'll be hard at work coloring in short order—but they'll be coloring the mahogany cocktail table. Save yourself the agony and expense.

## ♦ 453  Don't go bananas buying toys and clothes for your children.

Some parents are determined that their children have the fanciest toys and the dressiest clothes. These items are cute and expensive. Not only will such indulgences send bad signals to your children about spending money, they're also a needless expense. You should be less concerned about spending money on your children and more concerned about saving it for their (and your) future.

## ♦ 454  Get hand-me-down toys from relatives and friends.

If you put out the word that you are in the market for used toys, you'll end up with a roomful of toys from family and friends. Why? For some reason, when our kids have outgrown their toys, we usually put them away rather than get rid of them. So the toys sit in the attic, awaiting a good home. What better place than the home of a child of a friend or relative?

## ♦ 455  Buy preowned toys.

If you think about it, toys are never used up. Usually the little rascals will use the toy for about two hours, and that's it. Check to see if there is a used-toy emporium in your town. Yard sales are another good source of inexpensive, barely used toys.

## ♦ 456  Buy toys that will last.

Some toys are just destined to be destroyed within a few days, if not a few minutes, of handling by a child's fat little hands. On the other hand, some will last almost for generations. When you're buying toys for a youngster, avoid fragile items that are bound to disappoint the young hellion when they break.

◆ **457** **Compare the cost of cloth diapers versus disposables.**

Parents know that diapers are a big expense. But while many parents enjoy the convenience of disposable diapers, they are often more costly than using a diaper service. Compare the cost of cloth diapers against disposables. Then you can decide how much extra you're willing to pay for convenience.

◆ **458** **Buy a secondhand swing set.**

Most families outgrow a swing set long before it wears out. The swing set often sits in the backyard anyway. With a little bit of effort, you could probably arrange to buy a perfectly good swing set at very low price. You may even be able to get one for nothing if you're willing to dismantle it and move it to your own backyard.

◆ **459** **Build your own swing set.**

If your family needs a swing set, consider building your own before buying a new one. Whether you start from scratch or from a kit, you can save money by doing it yourself—and it's fun, too.

◆ **460** **If you plan to have more than one child, buy unisex clothing for the first child.**

You can save a lot of money by clothing the second or third child in the first child's hand-me-downs. If the second is of the opposite gender, you'll be glad you bought unisex clothing for the child's brother or sister—unless you're comfortable with putting dresses on baby Max. (A bit of useless information hardly worth knowing: Your second child is likely to be the same gender as your first.)

◆ **461** **If you plan to have more than one child, buy quality clothing for the first child.**

Quality clothing doesn't need to cost a lot. But by spending a little more to get well-constructed and durable everyday clothing for your first child, you can rest assured that it will be used again for future siblings. This is far cheaper than having to buy another set of clothes for each subsequent addition to your brood.

### ◆ 462 Get hand-me-down clothes for children from friends and relatives.

Spread the word among friends and relatives of your willingness to help them free up some closet space by taking hand-me-down children's clothes. You'll get perfectly good clothing, and I'll bet some of the preowned clothes you get will never have been worn.

### ◆ 463 Participate in sporting goods and clothing exchanges for kids.

Many schools and community organizations are setting up programs that allow parents to buy/sell or swap sporting goods and clothing for children. Why pay for new skis or a blazer for a youngster who will outgrow them in a year?

### ◆ 464 Avoid buying or giving expensive dress clothing for young children.

I was in an upscale children's toy store recently, and I saw $100 dresses for toddlers on sale. Sure, the kid looks spectacular in an expensive Laura Ashley dress or a Brooks Brothers blazer, but these things will be worn only a few times, if at all. If you want to spend that kind of money on a child, buy a more practical and less expensive piece of clothing, and buy a U.S. savings bond with the difference.

### ◆ 465 Save shirt cardboard and other cardboards for kiddie crafts.

Shirt cardboard and other similar cardboards and heavy paper are marvelous for the activities of the younger set, including drawing, painting, and crafts projects. It will also save some money, because this kind of material can be quite expensive.

◆ **466** **Bring home scrap paper from the office so your kids can color on the other side of it.**

This may sound like a small thing, but if you've ever witnessed the amount of paper a toddler artist goes through, you'll find that the scrap paper can be put to good use.

◆ **467** **Make your kids a homemade ice cream cone whenever the ice cream vendor comes into the neighborhood.**

My mother used to pull the following stunt. She would always have ice cream cones at the ready. When the ice cream vendor came around she would whip out the ice cream and cones, and satisfy our cravings at a much lower cost.

◆ **468** **Avoid throwing elaborate birthday and other parties for children.**

While the parents get a big kick out of elaborate and expensive birthday parties, the children's pleasure is fleeting. You can probably throw a more memorable and thrifty party just by using your imagination to come up with some fun things for the kids to do.

◆ **469** **Always assume that whatever writing implements a toddler gets his or her hands on will end up adorning your walls, woodwork, and furniture.**

In other words, every writing instrument a toddler gets his or her grabby little hands on had better contain water-soluble ink. Toy stores have plenty of such items in stock. A small investment in some washable markers for kids can end up being a real money-saver.

◆ **470** **Have your children make cards and gifts for their friends instead of buying these items.**

There's nothing cheery about the price of greeting cards. These days you can become impoverished buying them. The homemade variety are more personal and preferable, particularly for kids.

### ♦ 471 Make your youngsters' Halloween costumes instead of buying them.

These days Halloween costumes cost as much as a new set of clothes, but the costume will probably be used only once. You can save a lot of money by making your youngsters' Halloween costumes. It's a wonderful project for the kiddies, and homemade costumes will end up being a lot better and more fun than storebought ones.

### ♦ 472 Have older children make their own costumes.

Whether it's for Halloween or another occasion, let (require) older kids make their own costumes. It will allow them to use their imagination, and at the same time you'll be saving money.

### ♦ 473 Cut the kids' hair yourself.

Nobody can get youngsters to sit still long enough for a good haircut, so why not do it yourself?

### ♦ 474 Take advantage of the child care credit.

Many working parents fail to take advantage of the child care credit either out of ignorance or unwillingness to do the necessary record-keeping. Remember, this is a tax credit, which means you get a direct reduction from your tax bill—so it is worthwhile to do whatever is necessary to take the child care credit.

### ♦ 475 If your children are two years of age or older, make sure they have Social Security numbers.

When you list your dependents—including your children—on your tax return, you have to list their Social Security numbers if they are two years of age or older. If you fail to include their numbers, you could be subject to a disallowance of the exemption as well as a penalty. It's easy to obtain a Social Security number by contacting your local Social Security office.

### ◆ 476 Pay Grandma to take care of the kids and take advantage of the dependent care credit.

As long as the grandparents are not your dependents, parents can take the child care credit for payments to grandparents for childcare as long as the amount is reasonable.

### ◆ 477 Child care credit is available for part-time workers or job seekers.

Contrary to popular opinion, you and your spouse do not have to be full-time workers to have your child care payments qualify for the child care credit. If one or both spouses work part time, the credit is available. If one or both spouses are actively searching for jobs, the credit is available. If one spouse works part-time and the other is a full-time student, the credit is available. If one spouse works part-time and the other is disabled, the credit is available. Never assume that you somehow don't qualify for the child care credit. Check it out.

### ◆ 478 If your employer offers a dependent care assistance program (DCAP), figure out whether the dependent care credit or the exclusion available through the DCAP saves more tax dollars.

The law used to allow you to take advantage of both the dependent care credit and the salary reduction into a DCAP. But as luck would have it, the opportunity to use the credit is available now only where DCAP-covered expenses are very low. So you need to figure out which results in more savings. Generally, the DCAP benefits higher-income employees, while using the credit is profitable for lower-income employees.

♦ **479** **Don't leave out any in-home expenses for which you may claim the child care credit.**

If your children are cared for in your home, you can claim a credit for the cost of what you spend on the caretakers. The cost of a housekeeper or maid qualifies for the dependent care credit as long as that person's services partially benefit the dependent for whom care is being provided.

♦ **480** **Let Uncle Sam pay for part of the nursery school and kindergarten.**

Child care credit is available for outside-the-home expenses that go beyond the day-care center. Payments to a nursery and kindergarten are eligible for the credit. But anything beyond kindergarten is not allowable unless some of the payments are for child care rather than education. Just when you thought you were getting nothing from the government, Uncle Sam subsidizes the cost of launching your child into the educational system.

♦ **481** **Don't give your child an excessive allowance just to "keep up with the Joneses."**

Just because the Joneses are spoiling their children with an excess of allowances doesn't mean you have to follow suit. If your child complains, and inevitably he or she will, respond with the magic words "We can't afford it."

♦ **482** **Put your kids on a budget.**

Make your children account for where they spend their allowance. If they become wise spenders, you will save money in the long run because they won't need to ask you for more.

♦ **483** **Encourage your children to baby-sit.**

Americans are birthin' a lot of babies, and your child can take economic advantage of the boomlet by setting up in the baby-sitting business. There's good money to be had because the demand for baby-sitters outstrips the supply, which, unfortunately for us parents, means that the price of baby-sitting services has risen.

### ◆ 484 Part-time jobs during the school year can help the family pocketbook.

As long as it doesn't interfere with their studies, part-time jobs during the school year can help your child develop valuable work skills and at the same time help meet the high cost of raising—and of being—a kid.

### ◆ 485 Encourage your high-school and college-age children to get summer and/or Christmas jobs.

Two benefits accrue when children get summer and/or Christmas jobs. First, they begin to develop a sense of financial and career responsibility that will stay with them for the rest of their lives. And second, the money they earn takes some of the heat off Mama and Papa.

### ◆ 486 If your adult children are living at home, make them pay room and board.

A lot of adult children are living in their parents' home these days, thanks in large part to the tough economic times we are experiencing. But if they're gainfully employed, they should be paying for the privilege. After all, it's costing you, the parents, your hard-earned money to provide them with home and hearth. It's only fair that they share the cost.

### ◆ 487 Select motels/hotel/resorts where "children stay free."

If you're planning to travel with children, be sure the various programs offered by the chains and resorts offer discounts for your children. These programs vary significantly and are subject to change, so a bit of research can be very financially rewarding.

### ◆ 488 Buy additional copies of this book and give them to your adult children.

The way I figure it, by buying additional copies of this book for your children, they will be able to reduce their living expenses, so that, in time, they won't have to hit you up for as much money. Therefore, if you follow my admittedly less-than-objective logic, by buying additional copies of this book, you end up saving money.

### ◆ 489 Invite grandparents to visit often.

Why? Because grandparents always bring presents, and they baby-sit for free.

# 16

## Pets

A pet is usually accorded the same privileges as any other member of the family. As a result, it is often just as easy to get caught up in a spending frenzy for our pets as it is for any other family member. It could even be worse, because Fido and Fifi can't tell you what they want, so you may be inclined to buy them everything you think they may want. Here are some suggestions that even an inveterate pet-lover could use to put a leash on pet costs without depriving their beloveds.

### ◆ 490    There's no such thing as a "free pet."

Don't be tricked into thinking that those free kittens come with a free lifetime maintenance plan. My cousin-in-law and her family were the proud recipients of a free dog of pleasant disposition and multicultural heritage. A fine pet, no doubt; but according to the family, he accounts for a major portion of the lease payments on his veterinarian's Jaguar.

### ◆ 491    Buy your next pet from an animal shelter (about $25) instead of a pet store (about $300) or a breeder.

It'll love you just as much, and probably cost you less to maintain than some rare purebred that probably has bad eyes and bad hips.

### ◆ 492    Don't own exotic pets.

They're costly to purchase, costly to maintain, and will provide you with all manner of unpleasant surprises. Your life *can* be complete without owning a three-toed sloth or a googly-eyed gibbon.

## ♦ 493    Buy smaller pets. They eat less.

Smaller pets are cheaper. Smaller pets are similar to smaller cars: They consume less and they may cost less to maintain. So unless you're simply enamored of Great Danes, anacondas, or foot-long fish, consider buying a smaller pet.

## ♦ 494    Don't buy a pet that may be prone to expensive ailments.

Some pets—such as golden retrievers—aren't endowed with the most robust constitution. Such ailment-prone pets can be costly to treat. So before buying a particular animal, make sure you have a good understanding of its frailties.

## ♦ 495    Get a "low maintenance" pet.

There's a lot to be said for a dog or cat that doesn't require a lot of maintenance. While there may be nothing cuter than a little fur-ball pet, imagine what it costs to groom the little cherub—not to mention the constant battle its owner has to wage against shed hair.

## ♦ 496    Limit the number of your pets.

A neighboring community just had a big brouhaha over a proposed ordinance that would limit homeowners to owning no more than five dogs. Five dogs! Don't go overboard on pets. You don't get any scales of economy or quantity discounts, and I doubt that five dogs or cats will bring you five times as much pleasure as one would.

## ♦ 497    Feed your pet generic pet food.

I think you'll probably find that your beloved Fido is just as happy with generic pet food as it is with the name brands. It certainly doesn't hurt to try out a few cans.

## ◆ 498 Don't overpay for designer pet food.

The marketers are always coming up with ways for us to spend more money. Now they've come up with gourmet pet food. Don't even think about it. Instead, ask your vet to recommend some economical yet healthy fodder.

## ◆ 499 Check pet supply stores for quantity discounts on food.

Don't buy pet food in small quantities at your local grocery store if you can find a pet supply store that sells pet food in quantity. Pet food by the case or large bag is generally cheaper.

## ◆ 500 Don't get into the habit of catering to a pet's taste in food.

If your four-year-old child refused to eat anything but gourmet food, how would you react? If your pet is a finicky eater, is it acting any differently? Of course we want our pets to be well fed, but catering to your canine or feline gourmand is both time-consuming and costly.

## ◆ 501 Have your pet neutered.

Do your pocketbook and the animal kingdom a favor: Turn your he or she into an "it" (this probably isn't necessary for sea horses).

## ◆ 502 Check your local SPCA for low-cost neutering.

If you live near a branch of the Society for the Prevention of Cruelty to Animals, check to see if it offers pet neutering. SPCA rates are usually lower than those of private veterinarians.

## ◆ 503 Don't let your pet roam free.

Letting pets roam free is just asking for trouble. They can get lost, and they can get into altercations with other pets, wild animals in the country, or worse, moving vehicles. This is unfair to both pets and neighbors and could eventually end up costing you money.

### ◆ 504 Curtail destructive pet behavior.

If your pooch or kitty is inclined to destroy things such as furniture, nip this expensive problem in the bud. It probably won't require a consultation with a pet psychiatrist, either.

### ◆ 505 Bathe and groom your dog yourself.

Do you send yourself out to a coiffeur or a coiffeur to give yourself a bath or to comb your hair? Then why pay for your pet's expensive professional grooming? Even the president doesn't go to that expense. According to Mrs. Bush, their dog Millie takes a shower once a week with a "high government official."

### ◆ 506 Buy pet supplies from mail order discounters.

Just as you can find good values in mail order clothing, so can you save money by buying your pet's food and accessories from pet supply mail order discounters.

### ◆ 507 When you go on vacation, have a friend or another family member house-sit your pet.

Boarding your pet can drive up the overall cost of your vacation. Find a trustworthy soul to take in your pet or house-sit your beloved. You'll save money, and the pet will probably be happier than it would have been in some "animal house."

### ◆ 508 If your pet is seriously ill, decide on a financial ceiling for pet health care.

Technological advances in veterinary medicine allow a variety of elaborate treatments, including chemotherapy and dialysis. While these decisions are never easy, if your pet is seriously ill, you must decide how much you are willing to spend to prolong its life. Don't let your pet's health care bills run your finances to ruin.

### ◆ 509 Take care of your pet.

As with humans, a good diet, frequent exercise, and regular checkups can prevent major health problems for your canine or feline.

# VI

# FAMILY FINANCES

# 17

# Daily Money Habits

The way we spend (or should I say fritter away) our money on a day-to-day basis, it should come as no surprise that there are many easy ways to cut back. Also, once we get our daily spending under control, we begin to have the confidence to look for more significant ways to cut our expenses. But first things first. Review the following suggestions to come up with ways to get a handle on your day-to-day spending.

### ◆ 510  Quit playing the lottery.

Lotteries are nothing more than a tax on the naive. They are a complete waste of money, and the people who spend the most on them can least afford to do so. You might as well throw that money in the fireplace. At least it will provide you with some heat.

### ◆ 511  Tear up your credit cards.

This is one of the all-time great ways to save money. I suggest you do it with great pomp and circumstance. Afterward, treat yourself to a special dinner, but remember, pay cash.

### ◆ 512  Put yourself on an allowance.

Allowances aren't just for kids. One of the best ways to get your spending under control is to monitor and limit the amount of cash you spend on incidental day-to-day items, many of which are unnecessary. Figure out how to spend your day-to-day cash, look at purchases that can be avoided or reduced, and then put yourself on an allowance. Start each Monday with a set amount of money that should last you for a week. If you run out of money before the week is up, punish yourself by having to spend the weekend without. Of course you'll go take out more spending cash, but at least your impulse to excess will be tempered by the realization that you've exceeded your preset limit.

### ◆ 513 Keep track of how you spend your pocket money.

This happens to me all the time: I start out with $50 cash on Monday. By Thursday morning I'm out of money. My first reaction: Someone stole my money. But the sad fact is I spent much of the money unnecessarily. Keep a record of how you spend your pocket money. It will help curb one of the biggest sources of waste in your financial life.

### ◆ 514 Make a list of the contents of your wallet.

Few of us will get through our lives without losing our wallet at least once. It's always a hassle. You'll spend a lot less time and perhaps some expense by keeping a record of important items contained in your wallet. It will make replacing and canceling items much less irritating.

### ◆ 515 Don't carry excess cash.

All too often, the extra cash people carry for "emergencies" ends up being spent on frivolities. You really don't need to carry a lot of cash. Keep it in the bank, where it can earn interest.

### ◆ 516 Keep a traveler's check in your wallet.

Do you always fear that you'll never have enough cash in your wallet for an emergency? You're not alone. Far too many people carry excessive cash for this reason. This only increases the temptation to spend it on not-so-essential items. One way to keep enough cash while reducing the temptation to spend it is to store a traveler's check (perhaps in a $50 or $100 denomination), to be used only in an emergency. By the way, a sale has not, does not, and will never constitute a financial emergency.

### ◆ 517    Carry only one credit card.

It used to be that having a walletful of credit cards was a sign of the good life. It was nonsense then and it is nonsense now. Most people need one credit card for convenience and identification purposes. But there's little or no need to carry more than one credit card. They carry fees, they're tempting to overuse, and it makes your record-keeping more difficult when you have to pay multiple credit card bills each month. Also, it's a pain having to inform so many credit card companies when you lose your wallet.

### ◆ 518    Use your ATM machine sparingly.

ATM machines are convenient, but do you know that they can be expensive? An increasing number of banks are assessing charges for each use of the ATM machine. Find out your bank's policy, and if you're paying for the privilege, keep your ATM machine visits to a minimum.

### ◆ 519    Maintain a sufficient balance in your checking account to avoid monthly fees.

Chances are your bank will waive its monthly checking account fees if you maintain a sufficient balance in the account. If not, you can certainly find a bank that does. It may seem like a lot to keep up the required balance. But compare that against the fees you'll otherwise be assessed. Usually you're far better off keeping the sufficient level to waive the fees than you are by having that money earning interest somewhere.

### ◆ 520    Reconcile your bank account.

Always know how much money you have in each account. Don't trust the bank to care the way you do about your money.

### ◆ 521    Put away your checkbook.

The greater the distance you can place between yourself and your checkbook (not to mention your credit cards), the less temptation there will be to write a check for something you don't need.

### ♦ 522 Don't write small checks.

Avoid writing small checks for everyday expenditures, particularly if you're incurring a fee for each check you write. Somehow, writing a lot of small checks makes it seem like you're not spending money, but it's just the same as if you paid with cash, of course.

### ♦ 523 Use direct deposit for your salary check.

Depositing salary checks directly into your bank or credit union accomplishes a couple of things. First, you avoid having to drive or walk to the bank or credit union to deposit the check, which may cost you both time and money. Second, your checking account is credited faster than if you make the deposit yourself; the funds are available faster. While you're at it, be sure to ask your employer to have a portion of each paycheck automatically deposited into your savings account. Remember, the only way you can financially succeed in this world is to set aside some savings regularly.

### ♦ 524 Join your employer's credit union.

Your employer's credit union can be a big help toward cutting your expenses and achieving financial security. Credit unions often pay more interest on their savings accounts and certificates of deposit than does the local bank and also lend money at competitive rates and with less hassle than other lenders do. You have nothing to lose by joining the credit union, and quite possibly a lot to gain.

### ♦ 525 Find other places to have fun rather than Las Vegas, Atlantic City, or the racetrack.

Gambling may be a lot of fun for a lot of people, but why gamble away more than you can afford? Even if you don't count yourself among those who have had unfortunate experiences in gambling, look elsewhere for future fun and games.

### ◆ 526   If you must gamble, plan in advance how much you're willing to lose, and stick to it.

People who enjoy gambling at the casinos or the racetrack without impairing their family's finances inevitably plan a reasonable maximum they're willing to spend, and then they stick to it. Otherwise you can bet on financial disaster.

### ◆ 527   Get a discount for paying in cash rather than credit.

Retailers usually have to give up 2 to 5 percent or even more to the credit card company if you pay with plastic rather than cash. In other words, they're much better off having you pay in cash rather than on credit. Often there is some room for negotiating a discount off the selling price if you offer to pay in cash—so that both of you come out ahead.

### ◆ 528   Quit participating in office betting pools.

You probably won't be ostracized if you plan to avoid office betting pools. While it may be fun, it also costs money, and you may be up against some sports junkies who are far more likely to win than you are.

### ◆ 529   Consider using a prepaid legal services plan.

It all depends on how often you need legal services, but if you have the opportunity to join a prepaid legal services plan, by all means consider it, because it could be a money-saver.

### ◆ 530   Take the scissors to your ATM card.

This may sound extreme, but if you find you're frittering away a lot of your pocket cash and you're going to your ATM machine constantly to keep the cash flowing, then say good-bye to the card. Always limit your access to easy cash.

# 18

## Insurance

Insurance is one of the best areas for many people to reduce expenses. But you have to be careful. On the one hand, adequate insurance protection is crucial to preventing the big expense of an uninsured loss. On the other hand, you don't want to pay too much for the necessary coverage. It's a balancing act, but you'll find a lot of ways in this section to assure adequate coverage while reducing your overall insurance cost.

Most people are overinsured in some areas and underinsured in others. So you may find that some of the savings you can earn from dropping certain unneeded policy provisions or finding a lower-cost policy by comparison shopping may be partially offset with additional costs of added insurance where you have gaps. Don't fret, however; without adequate, comprehensive, and continuous insurance coverage, you risk incurring an expense from an uninsured loss that could be financially crippling for many years to come.

### ◆ 531 Raise the deductibles on your insurance policies.

You can save hundreds of dollars by raising the deductibles on your automobile and homeowner's or renter's insurance policies.

### ◆ 532 Don't underinsure.

While it's great to look for ways to save on insurance, don't be penny-wise and pound-foolish. Many people are adequately insured in some areas but underinsured in others. This can be financially disastrous should you suffer an uninsured or underinsured loss.

## ◆ 533 Earn discounts by purchasing all your insurance coverage from one company.

Many insurance companies offer discounts to customers who purchase all their policies, such as automobile, homeowner's, and umbrella insurance, from that company.

## ◆ 534 Don't buy insurance through the mail without comparison shopping.

You may periodically receive direct-mail offers for life insurance from a credit card company, association, or famous TV personality. While most of these offers are junk, some may be worth considering. How do you decide? Never buy a policy through the mail without thoroughly investigating the financial health of the company offering it. Just as importantly, compare the premiums and terms of the mail-order policy with those of a comparable policy offered by your insurance agent.

## ◆ 535 Buy insurance from highly rated companies only.

It used to be a minor concern, but those days are over. Be sure to buy insurance only from companies that have high ratings from agencies that measure insurers' financial health.

## ◆ 536 Don't buy too much life insurance.

Many people purchase far more life insurance coverage than they really need. Unless you want to make your survivors the richest family in town, don't buy too much insurance.

## ◆ 537 Don't rely only on your agent to tell you how much life insurance you need.

If you are trying to sell someone a product, would you rather they buy more or less of it? While an insurance company or agent may be helpful, their estimates of your life insurance needs have never been accused of erring on the low side. Be sure to make your own assessment of how much life insurance you need.

## ◆ 538  Avoid life insurance for children.

When the new *bambino* arrives, you may be bombarded by people who want to sell you life insurance for tots. Often it's sold on the basis of providing a college fund through a buildup in cash value. You don't need it. If you want to use life insurance to provide Junior with a college fund, insure yourself and/or your spouse.

## ◆ 539  Cut back on your life insurance coverage as your dependents become less dependent.

For most people, life insurance needs decrease as their children get older and as the insured nears retirement age. Periodically review your life insurance needs, and if they are receding, consider reducing your coverage.

## ◆ 540  Don't get credit life insurance.

Credit life insurance—insurance you buy from a lender to pay off a loan or mortgage in case you die—is almost always a rip-off. If you do need the insurance, it is cheaper to buy it yourself.

## ◆ 541  Buy term rather than cash-value life insurance.

I don't want to get into the raging controversy over which is better, term or cash-value life insurance, but I can say that term insurance is cheaper in the short run than cash-value insurance, despite what the person who desperately wants to sell you a cash-value policy will say. If you're concerned about providing the most insurance coverage for the lowest cost now, buy term.

## ♦ 542 Buy life insurance direct from the insurance company.

Several large insurance companies are now offering both term and cash-value life insurance directly—no agent involved. While an agent-purchased policy may end up costing no more, the so-called low-load life insurance policies are generally far cheaper.

## ♦ 543 Buy savings bank life insurance if it's available in your state.

Residents of New York, Connecticut, and Massachusetts have two things in common: First, they live in states that are in fiscal chaos. Second, they can take advantage of limited amounts of low-cost life insurance available through savings banks to people who live or work in these states.

## ♦ 544 Get a life insurance comparison from NICO.

There are several consumer organizations, including the National Insurance Consumer Organization (NICO) in Alexandria, Virginia, that will provide an analysis or comparison of life insurance policies to help you find the best coverage at the lowest cost. Write NICO at 121 North Payne Street, Alexandria, VA 22314.

## ♦ 545 Don't cash in one life insurance policy to buy another one.

It is probably unwise to trade in one cash-value life insurance policy for a term insurance policy or another cash-value policy. If an insurance agent encourages you to trade in one cash-value policy for another cash-value or term insurance policy, remember that you're probably ill advised to do so. Don't trade policies in this manner unless you do your own investigation. Otherwise you'll probably end up making an expensive mistake.

### ♦ 546 Increase the waiting period on your disability insurance.

If you have purchased your own disability income insurance policy, ask your agent to quote rates on a longer waiting period, perhaps six months or one year. The waiting period is the time between the onset of your disability and the time you begin collecting the benefits. The longer the waiting period, the lower the premiums.

### ♦ 547 Consider paying your own disability insurance premiums.

While this may cost you some money along the way, it could result in big savings if you become disabled. By paying your own disability insurance premiums rather than having your company pay them, any disability benefits you receive will not be subject to federal income tax. This can make a big difference. On the other hand, if your company pays the premiums, you will have to pay income taxes on disability benefits.

### ♦ 548 If you have to buy your own medical insurance, consider higher deductibles.

Health insurance premiums have gone through the roof. Many people who have to buy their own health insurance are finding it more and more difficult to meet these skyrocketing costs. But there is one way to bring premium costs down to earth, and that is by increasing the deductible—in other words, self-insuring the first few hundred or few thousand dollars of medical expense. Check with your insurance agent or the company that issues the policy about increasing the deductible. You'll be surprised at how much it can reduce your premium.

### ♦ 549 Take advantage of discounts on automobile and homeowner's insurance.

You may qualify for any number of discounts available on automobile and homeowner's insurance policies. Check with your agent to find out what discounts are available and which ones you qualify for.

### ◆ 550 Do your own comparison shopping for automobile insurance.

If automobile insurance rates are competitive in your state, you may save money by checking the rates offered by several companies yourself, rather than relying on your agent to do so. (Remember, your agent may not represent the company with the lowest rates.) Devoting a little time can reduce the high cost of insuring your car.

### ◆ 551 Be sure you have enough homeowner's insurance to replace your home.

Don't wait until it's too late to find out you lack sufficient homeowner's insurance coverage to replace your home in the event of its destruction. Many people fail to increase their coverage to keep pace with escalating construction costs and/or real-estate prices. Review your coverage now and inquire about policy provisions that automatically increase the coverage each year.

### ◆ 552 Obtain replacement cost coverage on your personal possessions.

This is one of those areas where spending a little money now may save you a lot in the future. Add replacement cost coverage to your homeowner's or renter's insurance policy. If you ever file a claim, the insurance company will pay the full cost of replacing the items rather than the standard depreciated value of most policies. Replacement cost coverage doesn't add a lot of cost to your policy, but in the event you suffer a loss, you won't have to spend your own money to refurbish your home.

### ◆ 553 If you're a renter, obtain insurance on your personal property.

Only one in four renters has a renter's insurance policy. The other three must enjoy taking a big risk, because that's what they are doing. Renter's insurance is inexpensive, and it may well save you a lot of headaches and money later on.

### ♦ 554 Insure any valuables you are storing in your safe deposit box.

Did you know that banks don't insure the contents of your safe deposit box? If you store any valuables in your safe deposit box, you can obtain insurance at low cost by adding it to your homeowner's or renter's policy.

### ♦ 555 Store unused valuables in your safe deposit box.

Why worry about your most valuable (heirloom) jewelry for a minute more? Place it and other too-precious-to-use items in a safe deposit box. (It's safer and cheaper to insure.)

### ♦ 556 Obtain a floater policy to insure jewelry and any other valuable possessions.

If you take the time (which you should) to read your homeowner's or renter's policy, you will be horrified by the small amount of coverage these policies provide for jewelry, silverware, and other valuable possessions. If you have valuables, have them appraised and then ask the insurance company to insure them with a floater policy. I'll admit this costs money, but these are also the items you are most likely to lose in the event of a theft.

### ♦ 557 Inquire about discounts on homeowner's insurance that takes into account smoke alarms, burglar alarms, etc.

Many insurers are now offering discounts for homeowners who take protective measures against fire and burglary. Check them out.

### ♦ 558 Take care of your property.

Fix the hole where the rain gets in and prevent claims that could send you to the poorhouse. While you're at it, fix *anything* that could move in harm's way—a leaning chimney or a seesaw step.

## ◆ 559  Obtain umbrella liability insurance.

Lack of umbrella liability coverage is the single most common problem with people's insurance coverage. People who lack this coverage could, if sued, get wiped out just paying their legal defense costs. You can get sued for just about anything these days, and umbrella liability insurance offers considerable protection against that possibility at low cost. Umbrella liability insurance picks up where your homeowner's or renter's and automobile insurance leave off. This insurance also covers any of your family's nonjob-related activities that are unrelated to your home or automobile.

## ◆ 560  Self-insure.

If you are blessed with enough money to be able to assume the risks of loss, you could reduce your insurance expenses by self-insuring, either through no insurance at all or by increasing deductibles. But don't delude yourself into thinking that you can afford a big risk when in fact you can't.

## ◆ 561  Don't buy nursing home insurance.

Nursing home insurance is one of the most oversold types of insurance. Unfortunately, scare tactics are often used to convince the elderly that they need this coverage. While some elderly may certainly benefit from nursing home insurance, it is often too expensive in comparison with the benefits offered.

## ◆ 562  Avoid "dread disease" or other narrowly defined insurance coverage.

One major New York bank used to offer a life insurance policy that would triple your benefits if you died in a foreign country on a holiday. Others provide insurance for cancer victims. This coverage plays on people's fears and is grossly overpriced. You need good insurance coverage that will provide benefits under any circumstances that might befall you.

### ◆ 563 Avoid air travel insurance.

Talk about a pig in a poke. Unless you have some sort of premonition about a flight you are about to take, don't waste your money on this insurance. If you do have a premonition about an upcoming flight, take the bus.

### ◆ 564 Pay insurance premiums annually rather than monthly or quarterly.

You'll save money by making insurance premium payments annually. Insurers assess a service charge for payments that are less frequent than annual.

# 19

## Investments

One of the best things about living beneath your means is that you have money to invest. But as the material in this section shows, there are numerous ways to continue cutting your expenses in the investment arena. Why waste part of your hard-earned savings by paying more than necessary to have your money invested or, worse, making money-losing investment decisions? The key to investing successfully and parsimoniously is to take control of your own investments. There is no reason why you can't be an effective and efficient manager of your own investments, whether you have $1,000 to invest or $100,000 to invest.

### ◆ 565　If it sounds too good to be true, it is.

Don't buy anything that guarantees to make you money without having to work for it, to lose weight without dieting, or to grow hair where no hair grows.

### ◆ 566　Don't invest in anything you don't understand.

If the person who's trying to sell you an investment can't explain it to your satisfaction in one sentence, don't buy it. Even if you make your own investment decisions, never invest in anything you have difficulty understanding.

### ◆ 567　Don't automatically follow the advice of the experts.

They're often wrong, and they may tempt you to make big (and expensive) changes in your investments.

### ◆ 568 Be wary of anything "free."

Jonathan's Law: Everything that's free ends up costing you money.

### ◆ 569 Don't make risky investments.

Don't let a broker's sales pitch throw your investment a curve ball. Promises of very high returns are *always* backed up by very risky deals.

### ◆ 570 Buy no-load mutual funds.

I can't understand why people want to pay someone to recommend a mutual fund when, with very little effort, they could select an equivalent or better fund with no sales commission.

### ◆ 571 Buy mutual funds with low "expense ratios."

Before you buy a mutual fund, find out from the prospectus what its expense ratio is. The expense ratio is the total annual expenses of managing the fund portfolio and can include hidden charges that are taken out each year, including the infamous "12b-1 charge" that reimburses the mutual fund company for its advertising and promotion costs. Always buy funds with low expense ratios. The average is about 1.25 percent of the fund's value, although many have expense ratios of less than 0.5 percent. Others, believe it or not, have expense ratios of well over 2 percent, which comes out of your hide year in and year out.

### ◆ 572 Avoid buying mutual funds with "back-end loads."

Many mutual funds assess charges to investors upon the sale of their shares, particularly if they're sold within a few years of buying them. Although I hope you're a long-term investor, no matter what, steer clear of mutual funds that have "contingent deferred sales charges" or that assess other charges when you eventually sell your shares.

◆ **573** **Don't buy mutual funds just before they are going to make a dividend or capital-gain distribution.**

Do you want to pay taxes on dividend, interest, or capital-gain income that was earned before you made the investment? Of course not. But that's what you're doing if you buy a mutual fund just before it makes a dividend or capital-gain distribution.

◆ **574** **Be your own investment adviser.**

If you're in the market for a new car, do you ask a car salesman for advice? (If you do, you should have someone check under your hood.) No. You read all the available literature about models in your price range. Learning about investing is not only your best defense against aggressive cold callers, it's also cheaper than paying some bozo who's in the business for *your* buck.

◆ **575** **Use discount brokers.**

If you want to make good investment decisions, make them yourself, and when you do so, use discount brokerage firms. They'll save you a lot of money on commissions, and they won't call you at dinnertime to recommend that you buy "Nikkei put warrants" or some other get-poor-quickly investment.

◆ **576** **Combine your investment accounts so you pay only one "account maintenance" fee.**

Many people have far too many investment accounts: a little bit here, a little bit there. While you might not realize it, each of those accounts is probably being hit with an annual maintenance fee.

◆ **577** **Buy stocks in round lots.**

Don't get into the habit of being an "odd-lotter"—you pay dearly for buying less than a hundred shares of stock. If you find that you can't afford to buy stocks in round lots, you should probably be investing in mutual funds instead. There's no penalty for buying mutual fund shares in odd lots.

## ◆ 578 Reinvest dividends automatically through a "dividend reinvestment program."

Many corporations offer dividend reinvestment programs to their shareholders. If you choose to participate, the corporation will automatically reinvest your dividends in additional shares of stock at no commission. This is an excellent way to build up your investments without incurring the expense of a commission. Anyway, what would you do with the small dividend check other than lose it or spend it on something silly? Better to reinvest it.

## ◆ 579 Buy stock through a "dividend reinvestment program."

This is one of the best inventions since thumbs. DRPs, as they're affectionately called, allow you to buy additional shares of stock you already own without paying a commission. Some companies even offer shares at a discount. It's a nice, low-cost way to build up a stock portfolio with a small amount of money, regularly invested.

## ◆ 580 Ask your broker for a break on commissions.

If you do business with a stockbroker, ask for a reduction in the commissions he or she charges. Many investors, particularly active ones, receive a reduction in commissions just for the asking. The brokerage business is very competitive, and you may be pleasantly surprised to find that even a smaller investor can get commission reductions.

## ◆ 581 Don't let too much money sit idle.

Don't put too much in a noninterest-earning checking account or a low-yielding savings account. Put the money you don't need immediately but may need in a few months in higher-yielding but safe interest-earning investments such as money market funds and short-term certificates of deposit.

## ◆ 582　Don't put too many eggs in one basket.

Whether you have $5,000 or $1 million to invest, diversification is king. Successful investors spread their money around into a variety of stock and interest-earning securities. If you place too much in any single investment, you're either taking too much risk or your money isn't working for you as well as it could.

## ◆ 583　Use dollar cost averaging.

Dollar cost averaging is a marvelously simple technique to build up your investments through disciplined saving and regular investment. Dollar cost averaging involves investing a fixed amount of money in a particular mutual fund or stock at regular intervals. You can get the details in any investment guide.

## ◆ 584　Invest in companies that pay regular small stock dividends.

Cash dividends are nice, but they are taxable unless the stock is held in a tax-deferred account. On the other hand, small stock dividend programs, in which stockholders receive additional shares of stock in lieu of cash payments, are tax-exempt. Studies have shown that companies that pay this type of dividend often provide investors with attractive long-term returns that are tax-free until the shares are cashed in.

## ◆ 585　Buy U.S. Treasury securities direct from the government.

If you buy U.S. Treasury bills, notes, or bonds, you can save money by buying them directly from the Treasury rather than through your bank or broker, which assesses a fee.

## ◆ 586　Buy U.S. savings bonds.

U.S. savings bonds are a much better investment than they used to be. While you may be able to do better with other investments, U.S. savings bonds are a wonderful way to invest securely with no commissions. They can even be purchased over the telephone by calling 1-800-USBonds. Make them a part of your investment program.

### ♦ 587 U.S. savings bonds + college education = a good deal.

Buying Series EE bonds is a very smart way to save tax-free dollars for your kids' college tuition. (Check the applicable income limits before you give it the old college try.)

### ♦ 588 Invest in Puerto Rican municipal bonds.

A lot of investors don't know it, but municipal bonds issued by Puerto Rico are free of both federal and state income taxes. If you're looking for double-tax-exempt securities, investigate Puerto Rican munis, as well as municipal securities of your own state.

### ♦ 589 Consider investing in tax-deferred annuities.

You don't save any money with your initial investment in a tax-deferred annuity, but this investment vehicle will grow free of taxes (just like an IRA) until you begin making withdrawals for retirement. The result, of course, is that you enjoy a tax-free buildup in the value of your annuity account.

### ♦ 590 Don't buy a vacation home as an investment.

Vacation homes are a huge expense, and many people buy them with the expectation that they will generate a lot of rent. Don't believe what is said by the people trying to sell you the home. Its rent potential probably won't come anywhere near their estimates.

### ♦ 591 Don't buy a "get rich quick in real estate" course.

You've seen them on late-night television promising endless riches by following their real-estate investment techniques.

Aren't they generous in sharing their knowledge for a mere $200? If you want to make money in this way, write one of these courses and go on television instead.

## ♦ 592 Don't invest in condominiums for rental purposes.

It's virtually impossible to fetch enough rent to carry the costs of a condominium. Also, condominiums have tended not to rise as much in buoyant real-estate markets and to devalue more significantly in declining real-estate markets. As a result, many who bought condominiums for investment purposes are hurting.

## ♦ 593 Don't invest in a single-family home for rental purposes.

While a single-family home may have more appreciation potential than a condominium, you'll never be able to get enough rent to cover your costs, even if you're able to enjoy some tax loss benefits from your rental property. What kind of investment requires you to take money out of your own pocket to sustain it? That is exactly what happens with most single-family home rental property.

## ♦ 594 Never pay more than seven times gross annual rental revenue for real-estate investment.

Just take my word for it. If you pay more than seven times gross annual rental on a property, you're going to suffer negative cash flows, which is a fancy way of saying that you're going to have to keep pouring money into the deal. What does seven times gross annual rental mean? That $140,000 condominium you want to buy for investment purpose would have to generate at least $20,000 in annual rent to have any hope of covering costs ($140,000 costs divided by $20,000 annual rent equal the amount of seven times annual rent). Those of us who fancy ourselves real-estate investors should take a lesson from the pros in this business. They never pay more than five to seven times gross rental for a property.

## ♦ 595 If you own rental property, take the steps necessary to qualify as an "active manager."

The requirements for "active management" are not onerous. They basically require that you make the decisions on important matters regarding the property's operation. If you qualify as an active manager and your income falls within certain limitations, you can deduct a percentage of losses associated with your rental property.

## ♦ 596 Contribute to an IRA and other retirement-oriented plans.

Obviously this doesn't save you money up front, but since the income from these investments is not taxed until you retire, it will save you taxes year in and year out. You need to contribute to these plans anyway if you want to retire comfortably.

## ♦ 597 Use capital losses to offset capital gains.

Unless you're an investment genius, chances are you have a few losing investments. If you have taken capital gains, you may want to review these dogs and take some capital losses. These capital losses will offset your capital gains and therefore could lower your tax bill.

## ♦ 598 Don't run afoul of the "wash sale" rules.

If you sell stock for a tax loss and then buy it back within thirty days, you will not be able to take a tax loss on the sale. Be sure you understand the "wash sale" rules.

## ♦ 599 Keep records of your investment-related expenses.

While investment expenses are subject to the 2 percent of the adjusted gross income threshold, you never know when you might have enough of these miscellaneous itemized deductions to go over the hurdle. Therefore you should keep records of such investment-related expenses as subscriptions to investment publications, safe deposit box rentals, fees charged by investment advisers, and, in many instances, the cost of travel associated with your investment activities.

## ◆ 600    Join an investment club.

Investment clubs are a great way to learn about investments so you can take more control over your own financial future. By sharing ideas and experiences, you will be able to manage your own investments more efficiently and effectively.

## ◆ 601    Go to free investment seminars.

What have you got to lose by attending a free investment seminar? The price is certainly right, and many of them are offered by reputable investment firms that would like to get you as a client. You're under no obligation to do business with them.

## ◆ 602    Avoid buying investment newsletters.

Most investment letters aren't worth the paper they are written on.

## ◆ 603    Invest some spare, college-earmarked money in your child's name.

Please note that I said "some." Don't go overboard on this, but if you can comfortably afford it, you might as well take advantage of the tax breaks for a small amount of money invested in the child's name, even a child under age fourteen. On the other hand, don't put a lot of money in the child's name lest they decide when they turn eighteen that they would rather do something stupid with the money like buying a car rather than putting it toward their college expenses. Also, avoid transferring any money to a child if you think you might qualify for financial aid. See tip #408.

## ◆ 604    Don't buy investment software and quotation services unless you know you are going to use them.

There comes a time in every investor's life when he or she fancies himself or herself a Wall Street tycoon. And any Wall

Street tycoon needs investment software and access to stock quotations. If this ever fits you, please realize that your ideas of grandeur are likely to pass relatively fast—so don't go to great expense buying services and software you're never going to make good use of.

## ◆ 605 Buy and hold.

You have nothing to gain from frequently changing your investments. The only thing you end up doing by trading too frequently is paying a lot of commissions that slowly but steadily eat away at your investments. The only time your family benefits from your frequent trading is if your son or daughter is a stockbroker—and one who works for you. Select your investments carefully, and then you should be able to hold on to them for a long time.

# 20

# Income Taxes

Figuring out ways to save legally on income taxes is as American as apple pie and baseball. Yet most people overpay their taxes because they are unaware of the many available and simple tax-saving opportunities. Many of the more commonly applicable tax-reduction techniques are described in this chapter. Numerous others appear elsewhere in this book.

By far and away the easiest and least painful method of cutting your expenses is to find a way to reduce your income-tax bill. It's found money. So review the following moneysaving tips to see how much money you can find.

### ◆ 606   Keep meticulous tax records.

Unless you want to pay more taxes than you have to, improve your tax record-keeping system. Have a notebook handy to keep track of miscellaneous tax-deductible expenses.

### ◆ 607   Prepare your own tax returns.

The best way to learn how to save taxes is to prepare your own tax returns. The IRS provides many free pamphlets, and there are many books on the market that can help you out.

### ◆ 608   Type your return.

Show the IRS that you take your tax preparation duties seriously. A typed return will send that message. Furthermore, typing your return will eliminate at least one reason for IRS agents to make inquiries about your return: illegibility!

◆ **609**   Increase your withholding allowances.

Are you sure you aren't having too much tax money withheld from your paychecks? If you got a refund last year, if you're going to have higher deductions this year, or if your income may drop this year, you may be able to increase the number of your withholding allowances in order to decrease the taxes withheld. It's not that difficult to figure out, and it's worth it if you can increase your take-home pay while staying within the strict IRS guidelines pertaining to sufficient withholding.

◆ **610**   Make your last state estimated tax payment (due January 15) in December so you can deduct the payment a year earlier.

As long as you are not overpaying your state taxes, state tax payments are deductible in the year in which you pay them. Therefore it may be to your advantage to make your last estimated state tax payment in December so you can deduct it in that tax year rather than paying it when it is due on January 15 of the next year.

◆ **611**   Don't overpay your estimated taxes.

Many people pay too much in estimated taxes because they don't understand the rules. Generally, estimated-tax payments—plus salary withholding—must equal 90 percent of your tax liability for the current tax year or 100 percent of your tax liability for the previous year, whichever is less. Therefore, if you expect to have a larger tax bill in the current year than you did in the one preceding, your estimated tax payment need total only what you paid in the previous year.

◆ **612**   Take advantage of tax breaks available if you provide substantial financial support to your parents or other family members.

If you provide substantial financial support to your parents or other family members, you may be entitled to take an exemption for them and also may be able to take advantage of other tax breaks.

♦ **613** **Request IRS Publication 17.**

Call or write the IRS to request a copy of IRS Publication 17, *Your Federal Income Tax.* This is an excellent source on how best to prepare your tax return. You may well find Publication 17 informative and thorough enough to make purchasing other tax preparation guides unnecessary.

♦ **614** **Avoid the "kiddie tax" by investing money owned by children under age fourteen in securities that are tax-deferred until after the children's fourteenth birthday.**

If you have a child who has accumulated sufficient investments to expose him or her to the kiddie tax—essentially taxed at the parents' tax rate—invest the child's money in tax-deferrable investments such as U.S. savings bonds. With savings bonds you can postpone recognition of the tax on the accrued interest until after Junior is fourteen.

♦ **615** **Plan carefully if you provide your parents with support.**

While the rules may seem complicated, careful planning can result in tax savings if you provide financial support to your parents. So trudge through the regulations to derive the most benefit from being such a good child.

♦ **616** **Plan carefully so you can claim the dependency exemption for children in college.**

Generally you can claim a dependency exemption for children in college for whom you provide over half the support, as long as they do not reach age twenty-four during the current tax year. Those who are over twenty-four can be claimed as an exemption only if their income is under a prescribed amount. Be sure to understand the relevant IRS rules so you can claim any exemption to which you are entitled.

### ◆ 617 Check before year end to make sure you are providing more than half of the support of dependents.

There are a variety of potential tax advantages when you provide more than half of a dependent's support. Falling just a few bucks short of the 50 percent support rule could cost you dearly, so as part of your year-end tax planning, put pencil to paper to make sure you will in fact provide over half of the support of, say, an aged parent. If it looks like you'll fall a bit short, you will have some time to make up the difference by, perhaps, providing a little extra living expenses or a particularly expensive holiday gift.

### ◆ 618 The dependent-care credit is available for care associated with disabled parents who live with you.

If you live with a disabled parent or child and hire someone to take care of him or her while you work, the in-home payments to the caregiver are allowable for the dependent-care credit. Unfortunately, if the disabled parent or child has to be placed in a nursing home or other facility, most payments do not qualify for the dependent-care credit. Even though payments to a nursing home or institution don't qualify for the dependent-care credit, they're generally acceptable as medical expense deductions and will be deductible if paid by you when they exceed 7.5 percent of your adjusted gross income.

### ◆ 619 Make a charitable donation of stock that has appreciated in value rather than cash.

If you donate stock that has appreciated in value to charity, you get a deduction for the current market value of the stock—thereby avoiding any capital-gains tax. This is an attractive moneysaving maneuver that is far better than donating an equivalent amount of cash.

### ◆ 620 Never donate stock or real estate that has declined in value since you bought it.

While it makes very good sense to donate assets that have appreciated in value to avoid having to pay a capital-gains tax, if you donate some dogs you have owned, you forfeit capital-loss deduction, since the charitable deduction is based on the current value of your donation. The best thing to do in these circumstances is to sell the investment, donate the proceeds to the charity, and then take advantage of the capital-loss deduction on your personal income taxes.

### ◆ 621 Take advantage of employer matching when making charitable contributions.

If you work for a company whose employer matches your donations to recognized charities, don't pass up the opportunity. In effect, for every dollar you contribute to a favorite charity, you'll be credited with a two-dollar contribution.

### ◆ 622 Keep track of auto mileage associated with charitable work.

Charity begins at home, particularly if you're setting out to do good work for society (i.e., charity or other volunteer work). You're entitled to deduct (as a charitable contribution) the cost of travel whether by car or other motor transportation associated with your charitable work. If you use your own auto, you can either deduct the actual cost of gasoline and oil (but not depreciation) or use a standard mileage rate.

### ◆ 623 Keep a record of all cash charitable contributions you make.

If you are like most people, you make a guesstimate of your cash charitable contributions when tax time rolls around. Unfortunately, even if you have underestimated the amount of your contributions, the IRS is wary of unsubstantiated deductions. So keep a log or diary of your cash contributions, or better yet, make all but your smallest ones—such as your gift to the March of Dimes—by check.

## ◆ 624 Donate unneeded clothing and other personal items to recognized charities.

If you have usable clothing, furniture, or other personal property you don't need, donate it to a recognized charity. You can take a tax deduction for the donated items' fair market value. Let Uncle Sam subsidize your generosity.

## ◆ 625 Don't participate in a charity raffle to get a charitable deduction.

Participating in a charity raffle sounds like such a wholesome thing to do you would think the IRS would award you with a charitable deduction. But the IRS considers these expenses to be the equivalent of gambling losses, a much less savory endeavor and one that does not result in a tax deduction.

## ◆ 626 Use certified mail with return receipt requested if you make deductible payments to charities and others late in December.

If you are audited, the IRS will scrutinize your end-of-year payments. It is wise, therefore, to send out deductible payments via certified mail. If questioned, you can then show your return receipts as proof that you actually made the payments in a particular tax year.

## ◆ 627 Use the envelope system at church.

If you put more than a buck or two a week in the plate at church, be sure to use an envelope with your name on it so that, if necessary, you will be able to prove the charitable deduction. Your friendly IRS agent is unlikely to believe that you plunk down a sawbuck every week at church.

## ◆ 628 Don't give money to persons or organizations unless you are genuinely interested in the cause and know your money will be put to good use.

We're always bombarded with solicitations by charities, some worthy, some not so worthy, some downright fraudulent.

Know where your money is going, and for heaven's sake, don't give in to some sales pitch. If you're uncertain about the legitimacy of a specific charity, check with the state organization that regulates them or ask for financial information from the group that so desperately wants your money.

## ♦ 629 If you have a full-time career and decide to go back to school "on the side," check to see if you qualify for the education expenses deduction.

The regulations governing education expenses deductibility are strict, but you may be able to deduct tuition, etc., if you are already well established in your career. The education expenses deduction can make the burden of the ever-increasing cost of higher education a little more tolerable.

## ♦ 630 Mortgage prepayment penalties are not all bad.

If you are lucky enough to prepay your mortgage, that in and of itself should be a big money-saver because you can avoid a whopping amount of interest. If you have to pay a prepayment penalty, there is at least a tax savings, because prepayment penalties are deductible.

## ♦ 631 Pay property taxes late in the current tax year, rather than when they become due in the next tax year.

You can reduce your current year's tax bill by paying property taxes due early next year in the current year. True, your tax bill may go up next year because you won't be able to deduct as much in property taxes, but it's better to have lower taxes this year and higher taxes next year, because you'll have more money available to invest now.

## ♦ 632 Ask the nursing home to break down medical versus custodial expenses.

If you are paying a family member's nursing home bills, be aware that part of these expenses—the medical portion—are deductible for income-tax purposes. If the facility doesn't already itemize your bills, ask whoever handles the billing to provide you with a statement of the expenses by category.

### ◆ 633 A "like-kind exchange" can avoid current capital-gains tax.

Real-estate tycoons take advantage of "like-kind exchanges" and so can you, although they may be difficult to put together. In a "like-kind exchange," a piece of property is traded for one of similar value. If the trade is properly structured, the parties making the exchange can avoid capital-gains taxes at the time of the transaction. A like-kind exchange may be worth investigating if you are interested in trading a piece of property rather than selling it outright.

### ◆ 634 If you loaned money to someone other than a relative and you subsequently determine that you will be unable to collect on that, you may be able to take a tax deduction for a bad debt.

Why act in a bankerly manner? The more professionally you handle loans to friends, the more likely the IRS will allow you to write off the loan if your friend or relative defaults. You must properly structure the loan at the time you make it and make reasonable efforts to collect it, for the IRS is wary of bad-loan deductions when the loan was originally made to a friend. The IRS will not, however, be able to repair the permanent damage that a dispute over money will do to your relationship.

### ◆ 635 If you suffer an uninsured or underinsured casualty or theft loss, you may be able to take a tax deduction for the uninsured portion of your loss.

While you probably won't be able to take a deduction for a small uninsured or underinsured casualty or theft loss, you may be able to deduct part of a larger loss. Don't automatically assume that you don't qualify—check the relevant IRS guidelines.

### ◆ 636 Shift some investments to children as long as the investment income does not put them in your own tax bracket.

While I don't advocate shifting significant amounts of money into your children's name, you could save some money by putting a limited amount of stocks or interest-earning investments into their name to take advantage of their lower tax bracket. Check the rules.

### ◆ 637 Postpone or accelerate payments of itemized deductions subject to the 2 percent rule.

The tax laws allow you to deduct miscellaneous itemized deductions only to the extent that they exceed 2 percent of your adjusted gross income. Check out toward the end of the tax year where you stand. If it looks like you will go over the threshold, pay as many deductible expenses as legally possible this year.

### ◆ 638 Maintain records of any unreimbursed expenditures for business-related entertainment and gifts.

It doesn't take a whole lot of effort to jot these expenses down in an appointment book or diary. The better documented your expenditures are, the more easily you can deduct them.

### ◆ 639 If you maintain an office at home, you may, under certain circumstances, take a deduction for the costs of maintaining that home office.

The IRS allows you to deduct a certain portion of the costs of maintaining your home if you have an office there. The rules are fairly stringent, however, so be sure you really are using that office for business purposes before you decide to take this deduction.

♦ **640** If you make unreimbursed business calls from your home telephone, they are deductible as miscellaneous itemized business expenses.

Keep records of business calls you make from your home that are not reimbursed by your employer. They are deductible as miscellaneous itemized deductions, subject to the 2 percent of AGI limitation.

♦ **641** If you use the standard mileage rate for business use of your automobile, you still may deduct certain other expenses associated with the use of your car.

A lot of taxpayers think that if they use the standard mileage rate, they can't deduct any other expenses associated with the use of their car. *Au contraire.* Several expenses are deductible on top of the standard mileage rate, including parking fees and tolls.

♦ **642** If your spouse accompanies you to a convention or on a business trip, you can usually deduct most of the cost of the hotel or motel.

When they are divvying up the cost of a trip for tax purposes, many taxpayers think that if the spouse shares a room, only half of the lodging costs are deductible. Actually, the business traveler is entitled to a deduction at the single-room rate, not half of the double-room rate. Since the difference between a single and a double rate is very small (indeed, in some hotels it's the same charge), most of the room charges can be considered as business expenses for tax purposes.

♦ **643** If you move, see if you qualify for tax breaks available to people who relocate.

If you move across town, chances are you won't qualify for moving expense deductions. You are eligible, however, if you are moving because you are changing jobs—or being transferred to a new location by your employer. One caveat: The IRS requires that your new work location be more than thirty-five miles from your old home for you to take the moving expense deduction.

## ♦ 644 The costs incurred while acquiring a home or finding an apartment in your new locaton may be deductible if you moved for reasons pertaining to your job situation.

If your move qualifies for tax-deductible treatment under IRS regulations, many of the costs incurred in the course of securing a new residence are tax-deductible. Be sure to check the fine print in the tax rules.

## ♦ 645 If you move, don't forget to deduct the cost of food and lodging on the day before moving and the day of arrival.

If your moving expenses are tax-deductible, don't forget to include in your final tally of pertinent expenses any food and lodging expenses associated with the move.

## ♦ 646 If you move, don't forget to deduct the cost of moving yourself, your family, and your car to the new location.

Many people forget to include the cost of moving the family, and the family car, in their total tax-deductible moving costs.

## ♦ 647 Keep good records of house-hunting expenses incurred in advance of a move.

If you and members of your family incur expenses associated with looking for housing (including transportation, meals, and lodging) and these trips commence after you have found your new job at its new location, the expenses will be deductible as long as the move qualifies for deductible moving expenses.

### ♦ 648 If you move, you may be able to deduct temporary living expenses.

The cost of meals (subject to the 80 percent deduction limit) and lodging for you and your family—for up to thirty days at your new job location while looking for housing—may be deducted as part of your qualified moving expenses.

### ♦ 649 If you are contemplating a move, be sure to become familiar with the "time test."

Delaying your move could be profitable. Because of the time test that must be satisfied for the taxpayer to qualify for the moving expense deduction, it's possible that by delaying your move a few weeks, your move could be tax-deductible. In some instances, procrastination may be financially beneficial.

### ♦ 650 You may be able to deduct your moving expenses even if you delay your move until well after you start your new job.

Generally, your move must take place within one year of commencing your work at the new place of employment. IRS agents sometimes grant exceptions to the "one-year rule," but don't count on it.

### ♦ 651 If you are in the armed services, or are employed abroad, special rules may help you postpone capital-gains taxes on the sale and purchase of a home.

The deadline for buying or building a new home to qualify for a capital-gains tax postponement is suspended for members of the armed forces who have been on extended active duty after the sale of the old residence and is similarly waived for persons employed abroad.

### ♦ 652 Take out a deductible IRA.

Would you rather pay Uncle Sam an extra $560 in taxes, or set aside $2,000, which will grow tax-deferred for your retirement? The choice is yours if you're one of the majority of people who qualify for a fully tax-deductible IRA. A working person in the 28 percent tax bracket who qualifies for the tax-deductible IRA saves $560 in income taxes by making a $2,000 IRA contribution. It's a deal you can hardly pass up. If you can't afford the $2,000, set aside whatever you can.

### ♦ 653  Take out a nondeductible IRA.

Even if you don't qualify for a deductible IRA, you can still save money by investing in a nondeductible IRA. How? Because the earnings on a nondeductible IRA (interest, dividend, and capital gains) are not taxed until you begin making withdrawals when you retire. Over the years, these annual tax savings can really add up as your IRA account grows.

### ♦ 654  Make your IRA contributions as early in the year as possible.

'Tis far better to make your IRA contributions at the beginning of the new year than it is to wait until later in the year, or even worse, waiting until April of the following year—the latest that you can make an IRA contribution for the previous tax year. Why? Because the earlier you make your IRA contribution, the sooner your funds begin growing, tax-free. Also, because the money you deposited in the IRA won't be generating taxable interest in some other account, you'll actually cut down your tax bill by making early, rather than last-minute, contributions.

### ♦ 655  If you receive alimony, you may be able to qualify for a tax-deductible IRA.

If you receive alimony but do not receive any earned income, the tax rules still may allow you to establish a tax-deductible IRA. Check the regulations.

### ♦ 656  If you are enrolled in a company pension plan, consider making additional, "after tax" contributions to it.

Some company pension plans allow employees to make additional, "after tax" contributions. Even though your contributions must come from "after tax" dollars, the money will grow tax free until you retire, so you will save tax dollars throughout your working years.

### ◆ 657 Postpone withdrawing funds from your IRA as long as possible.

Since the funds in your IRA grow tax-free, the longer they are undisturbed, the more they will compound. Ideally, then, you shouldn't withdraw a farthing from your IRA until reaching age 70, at which time the IRS requires you to begin making minimum withdrawals. If you are already retired, begin making withdrawals from your personal investment accounts before drawing on your IRA accounts, since your personal investments can be withdrawn tax-free, compared with IRA withdrawals, which are either wholly or mostly taxable.

### ◆ 658 Ask your attorney, accountant, or financial adviser to indicate on his or her bills which fees are tax-deductible.

Their fees may be all or partially tax-deductible. For example, professional fees incurred in connection with tax-return preparation or any other sort of tax advice or assistance are deductible. So next time, ask your adviser which of his or her fees are tax-deductible.

### ◆ 659 Vote down nonessential bond issues and other free-spending measures.

Don't let your state or town government take any more of your money through taxes than is necessary. While you may want to support some new spending measures, evaluate each one carefully. It's your money they're spending.

### ◆ 660 Decide carefully how you want to take your retirement plan settlement.

If you can choose between a lump-sum payment and an annuity when you retire, think twice. The decision has important tax implications. You'll probably benefit from discussing this with a tax accountant.

◆ **661** **Don't risk a hassle with the IRS if you pay tax-deductible expenses or make annual charitable contributions near the end of the tax year.**

If you make eleventh-hour charitable contributions, make them by certified check. When you pay by certified check, the funds are removed from your account the moment the check is certified. You won't have to worry that the recipient of your gift might not get around to depositing your check until the new year.

◆ **662** **Gamblers, keep good records.**

If you gamble, be sure to keep a diary and your losing betting tickets so that if you win big (an unlikely occurrence), you can prove past gambling losses over the year to offset your winnings.

◆ **663** **File returns separately (rather than jointly) if it results in lower taxes.**

Sometimes, married taxpayers will end up paying less taxes if they file separate returns rather than a joint return. Check the instructions on preparing the return to see if your situation may result in lower taxes. It doesn't hurt to figure it both ways, because you don't want to pass up legitimate tax savings.

◆ **664** **If you're owed a refund, send in your tax return early.**

File early. Don't procrastinate. Send in your tax return ahead of time if you're going to get some money back. After all, the government isn't going to pay interest on it.

◆ **665** **If you owe the IRS money, don't send in your tax return early.**

As long as you have paid enough during the tax year to avoid a penalty, there's no reason to file your tax return early if you owe money to the IRS. This is one instance where procrastination allows you to keep your money working for you until the last minute.

## ◆ 666 Amend your return if you overpaid taxes the previous year.

If you overpaid taxes in the previous year, amend your return and get a refund. But don't wait—there's a time limit.

# Debt

Unfortunately, millions of families overdosed on debt during the 1980s. Of course, they were just doing the same thing that the federal, state, and municipal governments were doing, not to mention banks and corporations. Make no mistake: Debt may have been "in" in the 1980s, but it is definitely *out* in the 1990s.

This section contains a myriad of tips on how to get your debt under control—if it is out of control—and how to be a better borrower in the future. If you currently have too much debt, you are doubly challenged to find ways to cut your living expenses—first to pay off your loans and second to build up a savings nest egg so you will never again have debt problems. It's a big challenge but a very worthy one.

## ◆ 667 Pay off your entire credit card bill every month.

Customer credit incurs just about the steepest interest rates of any debt. Pay your bills every month and spare yourself the finance charges, which are no longer tax-deductible.

## ◆ 668 Opt for low- or no-cost credit cards.

Several issuers offer credit cards at a low or no annual fee. In spite of what the ads say about "amenities," a credit card is a credit card. There is no justification to pay more than a minimum for the privilege of having one.

### ♦ 669 If you're going to run up credit card loans, use a credit card that charges a low interest rate.

When we talk about low interest rates for credit cards, "low" is relative. Most of the major card issuers charge nearly 20 percent, while other issuers, whose cards are just as good, charge much less. If you're going to run up a credit card loan, use a credit card that charges a lower interest rate. Each week *Barron's* provides a list of lower-interest credit cards.

### ♦ 670 Don't pay extra for a gold card.

You may be flattered to be offered a gold (or platinum) card on the basis of your credit standing, but you should ask yourself whether it's really worth it to pay the hefty annual fee. The words "Thanks all the same but I can get along quite well without your gold card" come to mind.

### ♦ 671 Scrutinize your credit card bills.

Mistakes can and do happen; be careful, as somehow they never work in your favor.

### ♦ 672 Shop around for the cheapest loans.

Although you may read in the papers that no one wants to lend money anymore, the fact is that loan interest is by far a major source of income for banks, and they compete vigorously with each other for the privilege of lending you money. So if you need a loan, shop around for the lowest rate and the best loan terms.

### ♦ 673 Borrow only for worthwhile purposes.

Good debt. Bad debt. Never borrow for unnecessaries. You're only going to dig a deep hole for yourself that may take years to climb out of.

### ♦ 674 Pay off higher-interest-rate loans first.

If you have several loans, pay off the ones with the highest interest first.

♦ **675** **If you need to borrow money for a short time, take advantage of the rule that allows you to withdraw money from an IRA account for up to sixty days.**

While I don't advocate taking funds out of an IRA for personal purposes, you are allowed to withdraw money once per year from an IRA for up to sixty days without incurring any penalties. If you need a short-term infusion of cash, don't pay interest to a lender: Withdraw funds from your IRA account. If, however, you aren't positive that you have the fiscal discipline to replace the borrowed funds before the sixty-day limit has expired, *don't* borrow from your retirement account.

♦ **676** **You can reduce your interest expense by borrowing against your life insurance policy's cash value.**

If you must borrow, one of the first places to look is to your life insurance policy. Cash-value life insurance policies generally have loan provisions with interest rates that are much lower than those charged by most banks and S&Ls.

♦ **677** **Consolidate high-interest loans into a loan with a lower interest rate.**

If you have a bunch of loans with high interest rates, consider consolidating them into a single lower-interest loan to cut down on monthly interest expense. Be careful with loan consolidation, because sometimes people end up simply adding new debt once they have consolidated their old debt.

♦ **678** **Extend loan repayment periods.**

This is not the smartest way to reduce your living expenses, but in a pinch you can lower your expenses by extending repayment periods on one or more loans you may carry. Remember, this lowers your expenses in the short run, but as you end up paying more interest, increases them in the long run.

### ♦ 679 Shorten the repayment period on your loans.

What gives? The previous tip suggests extending payment periods. How can you have it both ways? It's all based on whether you're concerned with saving money in the short run or in the long run. The best way to save money over the long run is to shorten the repayment period on your loans, because the interest you end up paying over the life of the loan will be reduced. The trade-off, of course, is that your out-of-pocket costs go up because a shortened repayment period means higher monthly payments. But believe me, over the long run you'll be happy to get these loans paid off sooner rather than later.

### ♦ 680 Maintain only one checking account.

Unless you can get free checking accounts, maintaining multiple family checking accounts only drives up your expenses. Of course, you may have to decide whether maintaining one checking account to save money is worth sacrificing domestic tranquillity. Often husband and wife want to maintain their *own* checking accounts.

### ♦ 681 Shop around for low-fee checking accounts.

Checking account fees vary widely among banks in the same community. You may find that some offer low- or no-fee checking accounts to attract new customers.

### ♦ 682 Make loan payments automatically from your checking account.

Many lenders will reduce the interest rate a bit if you agree to have your loan payments automatically taken out of your checking account. Doing so also saves you time and a stamp.

### ♦ 683 Get "overdraft protection" on your checking account.

Overdraft protection doesn't cost anything, and it can avoid the expense and embarrassment of bounced checks. On the other hand, some people, once they get overdraft protection, end up using the small credit line immediately so that they accomplish nothing other than incurring another high-interest loan.

## ♦ 684  Take advantage of state assistance programs available to lower- and moderate-income home buyers.

Most states have a variety of assistance programs that help lower- and moderate-income individuals and families buy a home. Check with the state to see if you qualify—it could be a real money-saver.

## ♦ 685  Make extra principal payments against your mortgage.

If you can comfortably spare the money, you can save a lot of interest over the years by reducing the principal on your mortgage. An extra $100 added to a mortgage payment could save you $100 or more in interest over the life of your mortgage.

## ♦ 686  Is your bank computing your VRM interest rate accurately?

Banks are notorious for miscalculating the rate you're charged whenever your variable-rate mortgage is adjusted. Get into the habit of checking and double-checking the rate to make sure you aren't overpaying.

## ♦ 687  Check to make sure you are not paying too much into your mortgage escrow account.

Periodically check your mortgage escrow statements to make sure you're not overpaying. Don't wait for the lender to remind you that you're overpaying—it could take an eternity.

## ♦ 688  Consider a biweekly mortgage.

Biweekly mortgages end up costing more in the short run, but they can save you a whopping amount of money over the term of your mortgage. Typically, you amortize your loan over thirty years, but instead of paying once a month, you can pay half a monthly payment every two weeks. This results in the equivalent of one extra monthly payment per year, so that your loan will be fully paid off in eighteen to twenty-one years instead of thirty. Biweekly mortgages are particularly convenient if you are paid on a biweekly basis.

## ♦ 689 Convert nondeductible personal debt into deductible home equity debt.

While home equity loans obviously can jeopardize your house if you get into financial trouble, they're the borrowing source of choice since, under most circumstances, home equity loan interest is deductible, whereas most other loan interest is now considered nondeductible "personal" interest.

# VII

# YOUR
# CAREER

# 22

## Your Job

If you really want to take the business of reducing your living expenses seriously, you need to look at every aspect of your life—every area where you spend money is a candidate for saving money. While you may not have thought about it in those terms, your job is an area that is full of opportunities to reduce expenses. Choosing a place of employment in and of itself can be an expense-saver if your employer provides generous fringe benefits. Moreover, the money you spend at work can often be reduced without taking a vow of poverty. Finally, by taking a positive approach to your job and by getting your personal finances in better shape so you don't have to worry about them, you will be able to do a better job, you will advance in your career, and you will probably make more money.

### ◆ 690 Brown-bag it to work.

Have you ever calculated how much you spend on lunch over the course of a year? Brown-bagging doesn't mean bringing alcohol concealed in a plain paper bag to your office. (Although, the way the economy is going, you might like a quick on-the-job drink now and then.) It means bringing your lunch to work. The total yearly cost of lunching out easily equals a month's rent or mortgage payment. Sure, your local restaurateur or deli manager isn't going to appreciate my telling you this, but I'm more concerned that you make better use of your money and achieve financial security. Bringing your lunch to work is a major step toward that goal.

### ◆ 691 Eat your breakfast at home rather than buying it on the way to work.

Whenever I see people stopping on their way to work to buy breakfast or buying breakfast at the company cafeteria, I figure they must be pretty rich, because they could save a lot of money by preparing their breakfast at home—even if they carry it to work.

### ◆ 692 Form a "coffee club" at the office.

If you find yourself picking up coffee or tea every morning from a coffee shop, start a coffee club with your coworkers. By pooling your money, you can buy supplies and the other paraphernalia necessary to make your own coffee at a considerable saving.

### ◆ 693 Bring your soft drinks to work instead of buying them from the office vending machine.

If you brought your own beverages to work (please, no beer) you would easily save $200 or more a year.

### ◆ 694 Order a large sandwich for lunch and split it with a coworker.

Rather than buying two smaller sandwiches, buy a large one and split it (along with the cost) with one of your friends. You'll end up saving a lot of money.

### ◆ 695 Buy a single group gift to recognize a coworker rather than individual gifts.

If you want to recognize a coworker (e.g., birthdays, new babies), you will save a lot of money by having everyone kick in to buy one big gift in lieu of each person giving an individual present.

### ◆ 696 When you start your first job, remember to take advantage of moving expense deductions.

The rules pertaining to moving are more liberal when you are starting your first job, so when you first join the workaday world, which includes the highly taxed domain of the full-time worker, at least you may be able to take advantage of a good-sized tax deduction.

## ◆ 697  Work for companies that have pension plans.

If you are fortunate enough to work for an employer that has a pension plan, you are indeed saving money that would otherwise have to be invested in your own retirement savings plan. Be forewarned, however, that just working for companies that provide employee pension plans will not provide you with a secure retirement. You will need to continue your own savings program to guarantee a comfortable old age. One note: Avoid job-hopping—it may cause you to lose your pension benefits.

## ◆ 698  Work for companies that offer generous disability and life insurance benefits.

Disability insurance is essential for all working people. Also, most workers need life insurance. The cheapest way to get coverage, of course, is to work for companies that provide disability and life insurance benefits. Even if you have to kick in some of the coverages' cost, you will still get a better deal than you would if you purchased life or disability coverage as an individual.

## ◆ 699  Buy additional life insurance through your employer's group policy.

If you need more life insurance, one of the first places to check is your employer's group insurance policy. Many such policies offer a covered employee the option of purchasing additional life insurance at very low cost.

## ◆ 700  Work for employers that provide generous health insurance allowances.

Health insurance costs are high enough already, and they're increasing at a phenomenal rate. It is very advantageous to your financial health to find an employer willing to pay a generous portion of your health insurance bill. Otherwise, as these costs continue to escalate, you will have to bear a heavy financial burden.

### ◆ 701 Encourage your employer to provide more fringe benefits.

You are better off having your employer provide increased fringe benefits even at the expense of a lower paycheck. If your employer provides these benefits, including insurance and pension benefits, they're not taxable to you. If you had to provide these benefits yourself, you would have to purchase them with after-tax dollars. With respect to pension contributions, if your employer does not provide a pension plan, you must establish one yourself and make regular contributions to it.

### ◆ 702 Participate in your employer's salary reduction plan.

Salary reduction plans, often referred to as 401(k) or 403(b) plans, are the wave of the future. You're very short-sighted if you don't participate in them. You get a tax break for money you contribute to the plan, the employer often provides some matching funds, and you can enjoy tax deferral until you begin withdrawing the funds during retirement; 401(k)s are simply too good to pass up. Unless you want to work in a fast-food restaurant after you retire in order to make ends meet, join these plans and participate to the max.

### ◆ 703 Participate in your company's stock purchase plan.

Look at this gift horse and pony up. Companies that offer stock purchase plans usually offer a bargain price so you have an automatic gain at the time of purchase. You have to be one sandwich short of a picnic not to participate in these plans. However, *don't* accumulate too much stock in your company. You need diversification. (I know of one ex-banker who lost almost all his savings when his bank went belly-up.) Participate in your company's stock purchase plan, but sell a portion of the stock if you begin to accumulate too much of it.

### ◆ 704 Get a college degree under your employer's tuition assistance program.

If you are lucky enough to work for an employer who offers a tuition assistance program, take advantage of this excellent opportunity to get a part-time undergraduate or advanced degree.

### ◆ 705 Avoid working as an "independent contractor" if you can work as an employee.

Many people think they're at an advantage working as an "independent contractor" rather than as a permanent employee, because they can deduct a number of expenses related to self-employment. Often, taking the "independent contractor route" can be a mistake. You will, for instance, have to pay both your portion and what would usually be the employer's portion of your Social Security tax, effectively doubling your Social Security tax liability. Furthermore, you will forgo fringe benefits that have a real cash value, benefits such as insurance coverage and paid vacations that are available to regular full-time employees.

### ◆ 706 File your expense reports regularly.

If you incur reimbursable business expenses, file your expense reports regularly. I know some salespeople who put off filing their reports for months at a time, thereby giving up the opportunity to invest money that their employers owed them. Sure, it's a pain to fill out those reports, but it's *your* money, and the sooner you get it back, the better.

### ◆ 707 Join a professional association to take advantage of member discounts.

Whatever your occupation, chances are you can join a professional association that will benefit you in two ways. First, you'll be able to keep up with important developments in your field, which will make you a more effective and, let's hope, a higher-paid employee. Second, many associations offer member discounts on a wide number of products and services, ranging from car rentals and hotel rooms to low-cost insurance coverage.

♦ **708** **Don't pay dues to a professional organization unless you plan to be active in it.**

Next time you need to renew your membership in professional organizations, clubs, or civic associations, think hard about whether you're getting your money's worth. Many of us tend to renew automatically, and then we never make use of the organization. Don't fall into that trap.

♦ **709** **Just because you are entitled to an employee discount doesn't mean you're saving money.**

Don't get me wrong. Employee discounts are great as long as you buy only things you need. If you don't need an item, however, I don't care how big the discount is—you're wasting money.

♦ **710** **Avoid job-hopping.**

People who change jobs too frequently can really jeopardize their long-term financial security. It may not seem so at the time, because many people change jobs to get higher pay, but in so doing they often forgo important accrued pension benefits. Even people who wait around to change jobs until they are fully vested will often end up with far less in their retirement kitty than they would have had had they stayed longer at a single company. Always weigh the ramifications of a job change, some of which may be very costly in the long run. Frequent job-hoppers must set aside much more of their own income for retirement purposes than must long-term employees who are participating in a company-sponsored pension plan.

♦ **711** **Find a job closer to home.**

While I'm not an advocate of job-hopping, if you are looking for a job, the closer to home your employer is, the better. Many people spend a lot of time and money commuting long distances. I knew a guy who lived in Staten Island but worked in midtown Manhattan. Every morning he walked to a bus, took the bus to a train, took the train to the ferry, the ferry to

Manhattan, and then took two subway trains finally to get to work. At the end of the day, of course, he reversed the process. If you have to change jobs, keep close to home.

### ♦ 712 You may be entitled to corporate discounts on airfares, hotels, and auto rentals when you travel for pleasure.

Check your company to see whether you are entitled to corporate discounts on pleasure travel. You may find that these discounts extend to employees even when they are not traveling for business purposes. On the other hand, even with the discounts you may be able to do better on your own. Still, corporate discounts are worth looking into.

### ♦ 713 Work hard.

Unfortunately, we are embarking on a new era of job insecurity. Layoffs and long periods of unemployment are going to become much more commonplace. It's going to be much more important to work smart and hard to decrease your chances of being let go. There's another advantage to hard work: The more you work, the less time you'll have to spend the money you earn.

### ♦ 714 Look for ways for your employer to reduce expenses.

While bringing your own expenses under control should be uppermost in your mind, you may well benefit, albeit indirectly, by looking for ways to help your employer reduce expenses. The more efficiently and effectively your employer operates, the better off both you and your coworkers will be.

# 23

## Your Own Business

If you already own a small business, you are undoubtedly aware of the importance of keeping business expenses to a minimum. If you are thinking about starting a business, you need to learn how to be a penny-pincher from day one. If you start out your business living high on the hog, you're doomed. So whether you already own your own business or are considering striking out on your own (but not striking out in the process), take the following penny-pinching suggestions to heart.

### ◆ 715   Think twice before starting a business.

If you are thinking about going into business for yourself, think long and hard before taking the plunge. Most wanna-be entrepreneurs realize that the majority of new businesses fail. What they don't realize, however, is that owners of failed or struggling businesses often end up wiping out a lifetime's worth of savings. So start your own business with your eyes wide open to the financial risks of being your own boss.

### ◆ 716   Prepare a detailed business plan before launching your business.

Take the time to prepare a business plan before starting a business. Business plans are difficult to write because they require you to make a very detailed analysis of how you intend to launch and maintain your business. But a good business plan will end up saving you money by avoiding as many financial mistakes as possible. A good plan will also help convince lenders of the potential value of your business.

◆ **717** **Investigate federal and state government loan programs for small businesses.**

To learn about loans for which your business might be eligible, contact the government agency in your state that handles small-business loans. Also contact the U.S. government's Small Business Administration (SBA) and other federal agencies that are responsible for your industry. You may well qualify for one of the many available government loan programs for small businesses.

◆ **718** **Structure business loans to maximize tax benefits.**

Be sure to understand the tax benefits or drawbacks of any loans you are contemplating for your business. Generally this is particularly important for small-business owners using a mixture of personal and business loans to finance their business. Proper advance planning (and the help of a tax accountant or tax lawyer if a large sum of money is involved) can assure that you get the maximum tax benefit out of your business loans.

◆ **719** **Work out of your home.**

One of the biggest mistakes budding entrepreneurs can make when their businesses are new is saddling themselves with too much overhead. If at all possible, start your business out of your home rather than having to rent an office with all the costs associated with rental space. Of course, some businesses, such as retailing or food service, cannot be effectively run out of a home, but all too often new entrepreneurs delude themselves into thinking that they have to have fancy digs. They end up regretting the decision later.

◆ **720** **If you operate a business out of your home, take advantage of the tax benefits.**

While you have probably heard that the IRS is clamping down on "office at home" deductions, if you are operating a business out of your home, you probably can qualify for this deduction. Like other tax-saving tips, you need to understand the current regulations and plan in advance so your home office will, in fact, qualify for the deduction.

### ◆ 721 Find low-cost rental space.

If and when you need to rent office, warehouse, or retail space, search around for the lowest-cost location that will still meet your needs. Rents can vary dramatically in a single locale and even on a single block. Avoid the temptation to rent in a higher-cost building. While it may not seem significant now, a high rent can really drag down a growing business. Look at it this way: Your customers will probably appreciate the fact that your quarters are modest rather than located in the land of mahogany and marble.

### ◆ 722 Negotiate hard on office rentals.

Even as a small tenant, you may be able to negotiate a lower rent and additional concessions with the landlord. Never take the landlord's first offer without trying to negotiate. How much of a concession you can expect depends on rental conditions in the community. In many areas of the country rental conditions stink, so the prospective tenant is in the driver's seat. You could negotiate free rent for up to several months, additional renovations paid for the landlord, a moving allowance, and even a cash payment upon signing the lease.

### ◆ 723 Ask sellers of used furniture and equipment to finance the purchase.

Individuals or companies trying to dispose of used furniture and equipment may be so anxious to get rid of them that they will agree to finance part of the purchase price. This may be just what the doctor ordered to reduce the amount of cash necessary to finance your new or growing business.

### ◆ 724 Consider subcontracting manufacturing during the initial stages of your business's operation.

If your new business involves manufacturing, initially "farm out" your product's manufacture instead of investing large sums on your own manufacturing facility. Delay establishing your own plant until you are certain there is a sufficient demand for your product to justify a major capital investment. True, subcontracting may at first increase your production costs on a per-unit basis. But that is a minor drawback compared with what might happen if demand for your product is sluggish: Not only would you be stuck with a warehouse full of widgets, you would also be burdened with a shop full of useless equipment.

## ◆ 725 Don't go overboard on office renovations.

Whether your office is at home or is in rented space, keep office renovations in check. There will always be time later, when you enjoy an abundant cash flow, to spiff up the office, but don't waste precious working capital on nonessential office renovations until you can clearly afford them. Instead, use some imagination in laying out and decorating your office. You'd be surprised at what you can accomplish on your own at a very modest cost.

## ◆ 726 Contact the SBA and SCORE (Service Corps of Retired Executives) for free advice.

Whether your business is new or already established, both the Small Business Administration and SCORE are excellent sources for free consultations. Why pay a consultant in a $1,000 suit when you can probably get free advice?

## ◆ 727 Inquire of local colleges about business school courses that require students to advise small businesses.

Countless thousands of businesses have benefited from enthusiastic free advice provided by a most unlikely group of people: college students. Many students enrolled in a business program are required, as part of their course work, to conduct a project that advises a business. You'll be pleasantly surprised at the fresh look these students will provide when analyzing your business problems. The only thing you must give up is some time to provide your student consultants with the necessary information. Once you've turned them loose to investigate your business problems you may well end up with some valuable free advice.

### ◆ 728 Suppliers can provide valuable advice on starting and growing your business.

Small-business owners lack the resources that large companies have to stay abreast of new developments in their industry. Don't overlook a marvelous free source of crucial information on just about everything that's going on in your industry: your suppliers. They have a vested interest in your success, so they are usually more than happy to provide their customers with advice on any number of critical matters. Their insights could well help put you on the road to success.

### ◆ 729 Join your trade association.

You will get more than your money's worth by joining the trade association that represents your business. If you are going to succeed in your line of business, you need to keep up-to-date with all of the goings-on in your industry, and your trade association is supposed to do just that. Once you join, be sure to take advantage of all of the services the association offers that can possibly benefit you.

### ◆ 730 Join your customers' trade associations.

As a small-business owner, you know more than anyone that you often have to spend money to save money. That's why so many suppliers join their customers' trade associations. It's a good way to establish contacts with customers and to understand their problems and oppportunities. So if this applies to you, join your customers' trade associations. It will be a very worthwhile investment.

### ◆ 731 Join local business associations.

Local business associations are a marvelous way to make valuable contacts that can enhance your business, whether through locating customers or by simply discussing shared problems with other businesspeople in your community. Also, many local and state business associations provide services that may benefit you, including low-cost group insurance coverage.

◆ **732** **Consider all sources of free or low-cost government marketing and product development assistance.**

If you're willing to do a little digging, you may uncover a pot of gold. Federal government assistance in product development, research, export assistance, market intelligence—the list goes on. All of these are available either free or at low cost. Many state governments also have facilities to help the small-business owner achieve success.

◆ **733** **Consider hiring employees whose training and/or wages are government-subsidized.**

The federal and many state governments have a number of programs that provide training and, in some instances, wage subsidies. These programs are designed to help handicapped, unemployed, and certain other categories of disadvantaged workers to find and maintain gainful employment. Many smaller companies in both the service and manufacturing sectors have benefited greatly from these programs, as have the employees.

◆ **734** **When it comes to professional services, be fee-conscious.**

Most successful small-business owners require the periodic use of professional advisers, particularly lawyers and accountants. Remember, your professionals are retained by you and are working on your behalf, so there is no reason not to show them from the outset that you are concerned about controlling their fees. Otherwise you may be in for some very unpleasant surprises when your legal and accounting bills arrive in the mail. So be sure to let your professional advisers know that you are concerned about their fees and that you need to be kept up-to-date on any work in progress that they are performing. Where possible, try to agree upon a fixed fee for a particular service rather than an open-ended amount.

## ◆ 735 Incorporate your business yourself.

When starting up a business, you may want to speak with a lawyer or accountant about the best way to organize the business—a proprietorship, a partnership, or a corporation. If you decide to incorporate, you can probably incorporate your business yourself. Contact your state government's division of corporations and request that they send you the forms necessary to incorporate. You will most likely have to file "articles of incorporation" or "articles of organization" and pay a nominal fee for your business to gain corporate status. Alternatively, you can probably buy a book that provides the information required to help you incorporate.

## ◆ 736 Do your own accounting or have a low-cost service do it.

So many small-business owners are so intimidated by accounting that they think they must use an accountant. Chances are you can do your own accounting, because accounting for a small business really isn't that difficult. In fact, you can do most of your accounting right out of the checkbook. A number of companies offer inexpensive "one-write" checkbook systems that will allow you to make accounting entries at the same time you make a deposit or write out a check. Alternatively, a number of inexpensive software programs make accounting easy. Therefore, while you certainly should be preparing accounting statements to measure how your business is doing, try to do it yourself first rather than hiring someone to do it for you.

## ◆ 737 Shop around for low-cost insurance coverage for you and your employees.

You never want to go without sufficient health, disability, and life insurance as a small-business owner. Even if it's a one-person shop, your business can usually participate in low-cost group insurance programs that provide life, health, and disability insurance. Your local or state business association, such as the Chamber of Commerce, should be able to provide you with information on these programs. Also, many insurance agents arrange for you to take advantage of group insurance programs for smaller businesses.

### ◆ 738 Select an insurance agent who will find the best insurance deals for your business.

A good insurance agent will not only advise you on the types of coverages necessary to insure your business properly, he or she will also do the work necessary to find the most cost-effective policies year in and year out. In short, find an agent who is responsive to your needs.

### ◆ 739 Negotiate for generous credit terms with suppliers.

Chances are you have the luxury of being able to choose from among many suppliers—and they realize that. Take advantage of competitive conditions by negotiating for attractive credit terms—you may get a better deal than the one the supplier initially offers.

### ◆ 740 Take merchandise on consignment.

Depending on the type of business you have, you may be able to take some or most of the merchandise you sell on consignment. This is one way to stock an inventory without using any cash—you pay only if and when the goods are sold. Check around to see if your merchandise suppliers will provide you with goods on consignment. Many successful businesses first started out selling products on consignment.

### ◆ 741 Look for bargains to stock your inventory.

As long as you feel you can sell the goods, check with the manufacturers of your products to see if they have any overstocks or discontinued lines. They may be more than happy to unload these items at sharply reduced prices. Let your manufacturers and suppliers know that you stand ready to help them out in their time of need.

## ◆ 742 Buy your business cards, stationery, and forms on the cheap.

Chances are you don't need to spend a lot of money on designing a fancy logo and on purchasing expensive business cards, stationery, and forms. You can get perfectly satisfactory printed items at much lower cost by using a mail-order stationery company or a local print shop. Remember, too-fancy stationery may send the wrong signal in the 1990s. Your customers want to know that you are as concerned about controlling expenses as they are. Engraved stationery printed on thick bond paper sends the wrong signals.

## ◆ 743 Encourage free word-of-mouth advertising.

Word-of-mouth advertising is the best and the cheapest. Do what you can to stimulate good word-of-mouth promotion of your business by first satisfying your customers, and second by asking them to spread the word about your business. You'll by surprised at how effective this can be.

## ◆ 744 Obtain free media publicity.

The media are always starved for good stories. If you can put together a good story about your business that will appeal to a particular newspaper, magazine, radio show, etc., you have a good chance of getting free publicity. Moreover, positive comments about your business in a column, article, or radio/television program is a much more convincing sales pitch than is the usual way of advertising.

## ◆ 745 Become active in your community.

Are most of your customers located in and around your city or town? If so, become active in your community. Potential customers who are aware of your civic activity are more likely to support your business. If you don't think so, check out the occupations of the people who are active in your town. Many of them will be small-business owners.

### ♦ 746  Cut your losses if your business is not working out.

If you start your own business, the odds are regrettably against your succeeding. There may well come a time when you have to evaluate realistically whether to continue your business. If you do find yourself facing this difficult decision, you may want to seek the counsel of an accountant or other financial professional. But you don't want to throw good money after bad. Far too many entrepreneurs, by nature an optimistic lot, have risked their homes, their savings, and most everything else to support doomed businesses. It is far preferable to cut your losses or, at a minimum, sharply cut back your business aspirations if the losses mount.

### ♦ 747  Purchase remnant advertising space.

Why is it that magazines and newspapers never have any blank space? The fact is that they fill any unused space at the last minute by selling "remnant space" at a pittance. Try contacting those magazines where you would love to gain some exposure but can't afford the advertising rates. Let their advertising salespeople know of your situation, and express your willingness to take some remnant space so that you stand ready to take it when it becomes available.

### ♦ 748  Purchase advertising space in regional editions.

You can advertise in big-name publications for a lot less than you think by purchasing space in regional editions. If your customers are located in a particular region, or if you simply want to advertise in a big publication so you can brag about it (not a bad idea in and of itself), check into the advertising rates on regional editions.

### ♦ 749  Purchase small-space ads.

While the advertising salesperson may try to convince you to the contrary, many advertisers have been successful using small ads, even classified ads, in magazines and newspapers. What you don't want to risk is spending a fortune on an ad, only to find out it doesn't work. So it is better to start out with a small ad. You can always work up from there.

### ♦ 750    Establish an in-house advertising agency.

This is one of the oldest tricks in the book. Advertising agencies receive a 15 percent discount from publications and broadcasters. But you don't need an advertising agency to take advantage of the discount. All you need do is establish your own "in house." How do you go about it? The absolute most you'll typically need is some stationery and a separate checking account with the agency's name on it, but you probably won't need even that.

### ♦ 751    All advertising costs are negotiable.

Think of the magazine's, newspaper's, or broadcaster's "rate card" as representing the absolute most anyone would ever pay for advertising. Do you think that General Motors pays the rates indicated on the rate card? No, and you shouldn't, either. Negotiate, negotiate, negotiate.

### ♦ 752    Barter your goods or services for advertising, if possible.

You may be able to find an advertiser who needs or can make use of your business's goods or services, which can save you *beaucoup* dollars of advertising costs.

### ♦ 753    Try cooperative advertising.

Many small retailers can save a lot of money with cooperative advertising. Large regional or national manufacturers, for instance, will often pay a cash rebate to local retailers when they feature the manufacturers' product in their advertisements.

### ♦ 754    Cut your advertising bills with "per inquiry" or "per order" advertising.

So-called P.I. and P.O. arrangements are available with many media outlets. These arrangements allow you to advertise with no money up front. Instead, you agree to pay a set fee for every order or inquiry you receive as a result of the ad. You probably won't get top-notch space or time slots with these arrangements, but the price is certainly right.

## ♦ 755 Bargain hard if you want to buy an existing business.

If you are going into business for yourself, you have two choices. One is to start the business yourself; the other is to buy an existing business. If you choose the second route, be sure not to overpay. Most sellers have an inflated view of the value of their businesses—just as we all do when we go to sell our homes—so you can probably settle for considerably less than the asking price. As with any major purchase, don't hesitate to walk away from an intransigent seller. Also, it wouldn't hurt to hire a professional appraiser to give you an objective assessment of the business's value.

## ♦ 756 Send out bills regularly.

Don't let your accounts receivable mount. It's easy to overlook or postpone billing when you're immersed in the day-to-day operations of your business, but collections are your lifeblood. Prepare bills on a regular schedule.

## ♦ 757 Invest excess cash in an interest-earning account.

It's amazing how many businesses let their checking accounts build up to ridiculous levels. The big corporations manage their cash effectively, and you should be no different. Keep enough in the checking account for your immediate needs (and also enough to waive service charges), but invest any excess cash in interest-bearing accounts.

## ♦ 758 Be firm in your accounts receivable collection efforts.

Don't let your customers take advantage of your good nature—it ends up being the "little guy" who gets paid last. So if some of your customers are stringing you out, be firm in your collection efforts. Don't worry about alienating the customer. Your business will never survive if your customers are unwilling to pay you within a reasonable time.

## ◆ 759 When you start your business, select the form of business organization that will be cheapest in the long run.

The decision to form a corporation or proprietorship is not an easy one. You may benefit from the advice of an attorney or accountant when you set up the business. One major consideration is to select a form of business organization that will be the least expensive in the long run. If you cannot afford to obtain professional advice, go to a library or bookstore to find one of the many available books on starting your own business.

## ◆ 760 Don't pay your accounts payable too soon.

Although vendors will love you if you pay your bills early, it only ends up costing you money. Set a file for your accounts payable so you will pay them no sooner than on time.

## ◆ 761 Negotiate interest rates on business loans.

Next time you apply for a business loan, remember that you might be able to negotiate an interest rate that is lower than the rate first offered to you. Often there is some room for negotiation, so it doesn't hurt to try.

## ◆ 762 Shop for the best terms and conditions on business loans.

Always remember that the business of making loans is very competitive. After all, interest is by far the major source of income and profit for banks and other lending institutions. Therefore, lenders are competing for your business, and you should certainly compare loan terms and conditions among various lenders so you can select the one that best meets your needs.

◆ **763** **If you are thinking of starting a business, try to get it launched before quitting your "day job."**

Bitten by the entrepreneurial bug? Try to get your business off the ground before giving up your regular paycheck. However optimistic you may be about your new prospect, more often than not, your projections won't pan out. So think of your regular paycheck as a life raft.

◆ **764** **Don't entertain customers lavishly.**

In the frugal 1990s, three-martini lunches are as passé as $100-a-head dinners. If you entertain customers lavishly, you not only end up spending a lot of precious money, you also risk sending your customers the wrong message. It's okay to entertain them, but be sure to project a "lean and mean" image when you do.

◆ **765** **Use independent contractors if you can legally.**

If you can use independent contractors, you can avoid paying the high costs associated with full-time employees, including Social Security and fringe benefits. But be careful: The IRS is clamping down on individuals who abuse the rules pertaining to independent contractors.

◆ **766** **Use fabric ribbon on your computer printer.**

If your computer printer uses ribbon, use fabric rather than film ribbon. Documents printed with film ribbon look handsome, but you pay handsomely for them. Your everyday printing needs can be satisfied economically by using fabric printer ribbons.

◆ **767** **Use a laser printer cartridge recycling service.**

Laser printer cartridges cost an arm and a leg. That's why laser printer cartridge recycling is a growth business. These companies can replenish your used-up cartridges for much less than the cost of buying new ones.

### ◆ 768 Send nonurgent faxes after hours when phone rates are lower.

If you are like most small-business owners, you're working well into the night anyway. So send faxes in the evening or on weekends, when phone rates are lower.

### ◆ 769 Use the backs of used paper for scrap paper.

In the old days, bookkeepers used to reroll used adding-machine paper so they could use both sides. While this kind of frugality may be a little extreme, there is certainly good use to be made of the back sides of used stationery, computer paper, and other sheets of paper around the office.

### ◆ 770 Don't print out documents unnecessarily.

Help save the rain forest: Don't waste paper by printing out documents until they are in final form. Some small companies get into the habit of printing out every conceivable item in their computer.

### ◆ 771 Buy office supplies at discounters.

Don't pay full price for office supplies. It's so easy to get handsome discounts at one of the many office supply discount houses. One isn't located in your area? Contact a mail-order discounter.

### ◆ 772 Consider employing your spouse and/or children.

If you own a business, there may be a variety of advantages in putting your spouse and/or children on the payroll. But be sure they really work, lest you cross the IRS. Still, it's in your financial best interest to keep your money flowing into the family coffers.

◆ **773** **If you miss the deadline for a Keogh, you may still be able to establish and fund a SEP.**

If you are self-employed or own a small business, you can take an income-tax deduction for contributions to your company's pension plan. A Keogh plan allows you to set aside more money, but it must be established by December 31 of the tax year in which you want to make a deductible contribution, even though you can delay making the contribution until the next year. If you have missed that deadline, however, you can both establish and fund a Simplified Employee Pension (SEP) plan until your income-tax filing deadline.

◆ **774** **Delay mailing bills to customers so that payment will not be received until the next tax year.**

If you've had a profitable year, you may want to avoid incurring more taxes. One way to accomplish this is to delay sending out bills until late in the year so payment will generally be received in the next tax year.

◆ **775** **Reduce collection efforts on accounts receivable late in the tax year to postpone receipt of income until the next year.**

Another way to slow down taxable revenue is to slow down on your accounts receivable collection efforts toward the end of the year. But don't let your receivables languish. It's better to collect these bills a little early and pay taxes on them than it is never to collect them at all.

◆ **776** **Pay business expenses in the current year rather than deferring payment until the next year.**

The more deductible expenses you can accumulate during a profitable tax year, the smaller your tax bill will be. To the extent possible under IRS regulations, pay as many business expenses during the current year as you possibly can.

◆ **777** **If you're selling assets at a profit late in the year, consider deferring the sale until the next year.**

Give some consideration as to which tax year is the better one in which to recognize the profit resulting from a sale of assets. If it is to your advantage to postpone the sale until the new tax year, by all means do so.

◆ **778** **If you're selling your business or part of your business, consider timing the sale so as to minimize or postpone taxes.**

The sale of a business requires as much professional counsel, if not more, as the acquisition of a business. Mistakes can have a very serious effect on the ultimate amount you realize from the sale of a business.

◆ **779** **If you expect your business to be in a higher tax bracket next year, accelerate the billing and collection of receivables into the current tax year.**

The rules are simple. If rising income will push your company up into a higher tax bracket in the next tax year, accumulate as much profit as possible in the current year.

◆ **780** **If you expect to be in a higher tax bracket next year, postpone deductible expenses until next year.**

If you expect to pay taxes at a higher rate in the coming tax year, it's only fair (to yourself) to defer as many deductible expenses as possible until the following tax year. In this way you will get more bang for your deferred-deduction buck.

◆ **781** **Contribute your company's stock to a charitable organization.**

By making a charitable contribution of "closely held stock"— stock in a corporation that is owned by one person or by a small group of people—you can obtain a charitable deduction without giving up any ownership interest. After you make the donation, your corporation will redeem the shares by buying them back—the only way the charity can really get any cash out of the donation. The rules are a little complicated, so if you plan to do this, by all means check with your family tax expert.

## ♦ 782 Use bulk-rate postage when sending out large mailings.

Many small-business owners make the mistake of sending out large mailings using first-class postage. If they used bulk-rate mail, they would save a bundle.

## ♦ 783 Buy used computer equipment.

Chances are that the computer equipment the big companies off-load will be perfectly suitable for your operation. You can get some very good buys on used computer equipment. Many computer dealers sell both new and used equipment, and, with luck, you might even find a dealer in your city who sells nothing but used machines.

## ♦ 784 Buy used office furniture.

Used, low-cost office furniture is in abundant supply. There's no reason why a small business needs to adorn its offices with fancy new furniture when attractive, preowned furniture is available.

## ♦ 785 Rent office furniture.

The last thing you want to do when you're establishing yourself is to spend a fortune on office furniture. Preserve precious capital by renting office furniture instead. Renting will allow you to obtain all the trappings of a nicely furnished office with little or no initial investment. But don't rent forever.

## ♦ 786 Don't keep too much on deposit with a single bank.

If your business is flush with cash, and I hope it is or will be, be very mindful of the limits on FDIC deposit insurance.

Generally speaking, you don't want to have more than $100,000 on deposit at a single institution. You'd be surprised at how many small businesses have had several hundred thousand dollars on deposit at a single failed bank. Devastating.

## ◆ 787 If you use your car for business travel, you can deduct unreimbursed expenses relating to the use of your vehicle.

Does your business take you out on the road frequently? If you use your personal car for these trips but are not reimbursed for the costs of operating your chariot, you may be entitled to deduct these expenses on your income-tax return. Calculate your deduction by using either a standard mileage rate or by keeping a log of the actual costs of operating your automobile during business trips.

# Commuting

Commuting is *the* expense no one thinks about. After all, you have to get to work to earn a living. Maybe not thinking about it is all for the best, because if you add up how much it costs you to commute to and from work, you might faint. Those who drive to work alone in their iron and plastic masters, in particular, are simply wasting good money— thousands of dollars per year. See what you can do to get your commuting costs under control by reviewing the following ideas.

### ◆ 788 Commute via mass transit.

This is the one biggest saver ever created, yet far too many people prefer to waste their money fighting traffic jams in their (usually heavily financed) chariots. We're talking big-money savings here, particularly for urban commuters. There is a myth that poor people use mass transit and rich people drive to work. If anything, it's likely the opposite is true.

### ◆ 789 Buy mass transit discount passes and toll vouchers to reduce commuting costs.

Savings from buying transit passes and toll discount vouchers may seem trivial, but they sure add up.

### ◆ 790 Join a car pool.

Isn't it a bit ridiculous to waste all that money driving to and from work alone, five hundred times a year?

### ◆ 791 Walk to work if you live nearby.

Do your health and finances a favor: Hoof it to work. A lot of people could, but they get into the habit of driving to work or to a nearby bus station. Short hops really add to the wear and tear on your car.

### ◆ 792 Ride your bike to work.

You don't have to be a health nut to ride a bike to work, although you'll be healthier for it. Unless the journey to work is unusually long, treacherous, or in San Francisco, try biking it.

### ◆ 793 Drive to work with your spouse.

Unless you work at opposite ends of the city or have significantly different work hours, what's the sense of both of you hopping into separate cars to drive to work? Isn't it worth trading off a little inconvenience for a lot of commuting savings?

### ◆ 794 Drive other people to work and charge them for the privilege.

You can reduce, if not eliminate, your commuting costs by forming your own car pool. You need not report any payments received to the IRS as long as they don't exceed your expenses. But I would recommend checking with the company that handles your automobile insurance to make sure you're adequately covered.

### ◆ 795 If you must pay to park at your place of work, look for low-cost parking.

Don't overpay for parking. You may have to walk a few extra blocks to get from car to office, but you could save money by using the cheapest place to park. Of course, if you have to pay anything for the privilege of parking, perhaps it's time to try taking public transportation.

♦ **796** **Leave for and from work a little early (or a little late) to avoid rush-hour traffic jams.**

If you can persuade your boss, why not ditch the timeworn nine-to-five schedule in favor of a slightly modified one? By working from eight-thirty to four-thirty or from nine-thirty to five-thirty, you can avoid all the costly annoyances that characterize rush hour. A smoother commute will reduce your stress as well as prolong the life of your car.

♦ **797** **If you work at two different places, don't forget to deduct any unreimbursed costs for travel from one place to another.**

If this applies to you, check on the specific rules, but generally you can deduct the cost for going from the first location to the second in the event you moonlight, for example. However, the drive from the second location back to your home is not deductible—it's deemed commuting by the IRS.

♦ **798** **If you are thinking of moving, move closer to your place of work.**

If you are settled in your job and your employer is settled in a particular location, moving closer to work is certainly a major way to save time and money. Commuting is basically a waste of both those precious commodities. The less time and money you commit to commuting, the more energy and funds you will have to enjoy life.

# VIII

# Leisure

# 25

## Dining Out

**"'T**is wine, 'tis wine, that makes the lover bold." Unfortunately, it also makes the spender bold, too. How many times have you gone out to a restaurant planning to have a light meal consisting of a reasonably priced entrée and end up having goose liver pâté for an appetizer, roast duck for a main course, coffee, dessert, and a couple of bottles of overpriced wine? It's time to get your dining expenses under control. After one night of good food, you shouldn't have to rely on TV dinners until the next paycheck arrives. You can get back to the basics and still find surprisingly good food. There are many economical ways to paint the town pink without ending up in the red, and this chapter puts them all right on the table.

### ◆ 799 Save restaurants for special occasions.

Americans are restaurant addicts. If you're inclined to pinch pennies, kick the habit.

### ◆ 800 Eat at cheaper restaurants.

There are marvelous restaurants in your community that serve good food, have good service, and charge a lot less than you're used to paying for a night on the town.

### ◆ 801 Get take-out instead of eating in the restaurant.

It doesn't have the ambience, but you'll save on tipping and you can provide your own drinks. If the take-out joint is close by, walk over and pick it up instead of paying for delivery.

### ◆ 802 Don't order more at a restaurant than you can eat.

Sure, you can put the food in a doggie bag, but that's a mighty expensive leftover that you're schlepping home. Don't join the "eyes bigger than the stomach" club by ordering more than you can eat. You're better off ordering less. I'm sure you won't go home hungry, but if you do, you can always raid the refrigerator.

### ◆ 803 Eat dessert at home.

As delectable as the dessert tray looks, resist temptation and have dessert at home. Desserts add a lot to your restaurant bill, so do without.

### ◆ 804 Avoid high-ticket menu items.

Ordering the most expensive items on the menu is no fun for your purse. So, as appealing as the Chateaubriand replete with fresh baby vegetables sounds, try to enjoy something a little more reasonably priced.

### ◆ 805 Take home leftovers in a doggie bag.

If you do find yourself with more than you can eat, don't be shy about ordering a doggie bag. After all, it's your food, and you paid for it.

### ◆ 806 Enjoy the "house" wine.

Most restaurants won't bring shame on themselves by proffering a lousy house wine. Since house wine is always a lot cheaper than a decent selection from the wine list, you'll save money and enjoy a pretty good wine.

### ◆ 807 Split desserts.

I must confess that it's difficult to pass up a restaurant's megacaloric chocolate cake (accompanied by ice cream, of course). I usually find that one member of our dinner party is more than happy to share my dessert. (Between you and me, I could eat four pieces of that cake, but I'm simply too cheap to pay for them.)

### ◆ 808   Don't overtip.

I'm certainly not against tipping for good service, but I am opposed to overtipping. Fifteen to 20 percent of the bill (not including tax) is sufficient, unless you are at some high-class joint where legions of waiters fawn all over you. Frankly, I wouldn't know how much to tip in those places, so I avoid them.

### ◆ 809   Patronize restaurants that offer "early bird" discounts.

If you're willing to eat early, many restaurants are willing to feed you at a good discount.

### ◆ 810   If you're taking the kids out, go to restaurants that have kiddie menus.

Don't waste your money buying an adult meal for a child. Go to eateries that cater to the younger set.

### ◆ 811   Have your drinks at home before going out.

They're cost-quenching.

### ◆ 812   Avoid exotic drinks.

Unless it's your birthday or some other cause for celebration, don't buy fancy, overpriced drinks that come adorned with all kinds of unusual accoutrements, most often umbrellas. I've never been able to figure out why they put umbrellas in drinks—maybe to keep the sun from melting the ice cubes.

### ◆ 813   If you have to tip to get a table, find another restaurant.

If it's customary to grease the greedy palm of the maître d' to get seated at a dining establishment, you'll probably faint when you see the menu prices.

◆ **814** If you are a stranger in town, find out where the local service clubs meet for lunch.

One trick to finding a restaurant that provides satisfactory food at a good price is to inquire where the Rotary or Kiwanis Club meets for lunch.

◆ **815** If you are famished in an unfamiliar town, drive up to a drive-in bank and ask the teller where he or she grabs lunch.

It doesn't necessarily need to be a bank teller, but asking locals is a great way to locate good, reasonably priced eateries.

◆ **816** Don't hesitate to look carefully at the menu/price listing outside a restaurant.

Don't be embarrassed by checking the menu prices outside any restaurant—that's their purpose. This will also save you from potential embarrassment inside the restaurant.

◆ **817** When your waiter or waitress rattles off the day's specials, be sure you know their prices—before ordering.

There's nothing wrong with asking the price of the day's specials. It's far better than being rudely surprised by the out-of-this-world roasted quail's price.

◆ **818** Take advantage of "two for the price of one meal" deals.

Restaurants often use a variety of gimmicks to attract the hungry, such as two meals for the price of one. It's hard to go wrong with an inducement like that. One note: The free meal usually must be of equal or *lesser* value than the one for which you paid, so don't go in expecting to buy a hamburger and get a free duck à l'orange with it.

### ◆ 819     Go to an "all you can eat" buffet.

The best strategy for "all you can eat" buffet devotees is to skip the meal before the meal that you plan to eat at the buffet. In other words, if it's a Sunday brunch buffet, don't have any breakfast! Perhaps this isn't the most healthy way to eat, but it saves grocery money.

### ◆ 820     Take advantage of restaurant discount coupons.

To attract business in this tight economy, many restaurants participate in coupon programs that offer good discounts to patrons. Often these coupons appear in coupon books, which allow you to choose from among a variety of local restaurants.

### ◆ 821     Instead of ordering two small salads, order a large salad and split it.

This kind of togetherness can be a money-saver.

### ◆ 822     Go to a Chinese restaurant and share.

Most Chinese restaurants offer good value: tasty food in large quantity, and a very varied menu that can and should be shared with your tablemates.

### ◆ 823     There is such a thing as a free dinner.

There may be no such thing as a free lunch, but you can almost always find a bar that's offering dinner fixings—pizza, chicken wings, pastas, and cheese and crackers—for free. The reason? They're fishing for your patronage with free food as their lure. So the next time you want to eat out but your budget wants you to eat in, drive to a nearby tavern (usually between the hours of five and seven) and eat—if you must drink, have a draft beer—and be merry.

### ◆ 824     Never run up a tab on drinks.

You could be in for a rude awakening when an astronomical bar tab is presented. It's better to pay when each drink is served.

### ◆ 825 Eat at a fancy restaurant's café.

The food's the same, but the prices are much lower.

### ◆ 826 Go to the bar of a fancy restaurant.

You can be seen but not impoverished.

### ◆ 827 Become a "regular."

Restaurant regulars often get some sort of perks that save money—such as free drinks.

# 26

## Entertainment

There's no business like show business—your wallet can attest to that. Paying full price for movies, videos, tapes, and CDs, let alone for theater and symphony tickets, could bankrupt even a thrifty New Englander like myself. Back in the seventeenth century, when the Puritans called the shots up here, theatrical performances were banned, ostensibly for moral reasons, but really because religious leaders were afraid people would bankrupt themselves buying tickets to road productions of *Volpone*.

There's hope, however: There are several ways to cut your entertainment expenses without sacrificing quality. Discount movie passes, free concerts, free videos, and parties that let you entertain while your saving account relaxes are just some of the suggestions that follow.

### ◆ 828 Rent movies instead of going out to the movies.

Unless you feel compelled to see the latest movies, rent them and bring them home. Have you noticed that movie theater ticket prices keep rising and movie rental prices keep dropping? That's entertainment.

### ◆ 829 Subscribe to fewer stations or cancel your cable service altogether.

Television is a necessity and it can be a welcome diversion, but do you need 350 channels?

◆ **830** **Cancel subscriptions to newspapers or magazines you don't read.**

If you don't read it, you don't need it.

◆ **831** **Swap magazines with friends.**

Set up a magazine swapping group.

◆ **832** **Make better use of your library.**

My publisher won't like me to say this, but you can save money by checking books you want to read out of the library rather than buying them. Sadly, libraries are one of our most overlooked resources. If you haven't seen the inside of a library in a while, check it out. You'll be surprised at the many resources that are yours just for the asking.

◆ **833** **Borrow and/or trade videos with friends and acquaintances.**

Make sure to ask friends and acquaintances about their video-tape collections. You may find out that they have some tapes you would like to see and vice versa.

◆ **834** **Get videos at the library.**

A lot of people don't know that they can get videos at their local library. Is there any earthly reason why you'd want to pay to rent a video if it's available—at no cost—at your library?

◆ **835** **Get records, tapes, and compact discs at the library.**

Music freaks probably abhor the quietude of a library. They'd rather have music blasting from their eight-speaker system. But it may be worth visiting a quiet place to investigate their collection of records, tapes, and compact discs.

◆ **836** **Plan in advance to make a lot of ice before a party rather than having to buy it.**

There must be a lot of money in ice. You freeze water and then sell it to ill-prepared party throwers. With a little advance planning, you can make enough ice to suit the whole crowd.

### ◆ 837 Throw potluck parties.

Why go to the expense and effort of throwing a dinner party when you can have a lot of fun hosting a potluck dinner? In that way everyone can contribute something to the soiree. A word to the wise: If you invite any bachelors to the party, don't risk asking them to bring prepared food. It'll be safer for all concerned to have them contribute napkins, paper plates, plastic cutlery, or potato chips.

### ◆ 838 Throw BYOB parties.

Next time you're having a large group over, ask your guests to bring their own bottle. You can save a lot of money; and if your friends are into wine, you'll probably get the chance to sample some interesting vintages.

### ◆ 839 Go to the movies when ticket prices are reduced.

Ask your local movie theaters if they reduce their ticket prices at certain times of the day or days of the week. Don't worry, if they knock 40 percent off the ticket prices they won't shorten the movie by 40 percent.

### ◆ 840 Don't buy candy or soft drinks at the theater or ball park.

You can easily spend the price of a ticket on food at a theater or athletic event. (Wouldn't you love to own the concession?) Either go to the theater or ball park with a full belly, or bring along a snack. While they may not let you bring a food cart in to feed you and the kiddies, there's nothing wrong with packing a snack.

### ◆ 841 Go to matinees.

Instead of making an evening of theater entertainment, why not make an afternoon of entertainment and save some

money in the process? Most theaters offer matinees at reduced prices so you can see the play you've been wanting to
see without having to take out a home equity loan to pay
evening theater prices.

### ◆ 842  Usher at the theater.

This is for the real penny-pinching culture freaks. Inquire
about working as an usher so you can max out on movies,
concerts, or whatever strikes your fancy.

### ◆ 843  Take advantage of free concerts.

Check your local newspaper for listings of free concerts in
your community. A great way to have a pleasant time at just
the right price.

### ◆ 844  Join a concert series or buy season tick-
ets.

If you're really into the theater, symphony, or a local sports
team, consider buying season tickets. You can usually get
them at a reduced price, and in addition, you'll probably get
better seat location. If you can't make it for every concert or
game, consider splitting your tickets with friends who are
similarly devoted to the symphonic, dramatic, or athletic life.

### ◆ 845  Pack lunches for family excursions.

If the family is going out for a day of fun and games, why not
pack a meal? You can certainly put something together that's
more nutritious than the fare offered by the fast-food joints,
and it'll be a lot cheaper.

### ◆ 846  Take advantage of outdoor free or inex-
pensive entertainment in the summer.

There's a lot of free or inexpensive entertainment that most
of us are either not aware of or don't take enough advantage
of. It can range from community-sponsored concerts and fairs
to informal gatherings of musicians, mimes, or jugglers on
the streets of our cities or college towns. Some of the latter is

quite good and some is downright awful, but it's all worth the price of admission: nothing. Never, never, never feel that you have to pay a lot to be entertained. We're a nation of entertainers; you need only go out on the street to witness all manner of it.

### ♦ 847 Resign from any social or country clubs you don't use frequently.

Some people pay a lot of money to belong to clubs they don't use frequently. It's a waste of money. Think about it. If you pay $400 in dues and use the club once a year for a $50 dinner, haven't you had a $450 dinner? And a pretty mediocre one at that.

### ♦ 848 Ask for bulk discounts at your video store.

Why pay $2.50 when $1.00 will do? Find out if your local video store offers discounts to customers who rent frequently. If the store doesn't offer a discount program, ask them to consider establishing one.

### ♦ 849 Take advantage of your video store's slow days.

Many video stores offer discounts on slow rental days, typically Mondays and Tuesdays. So mark your calendar and make those nights your movie nights.

### ♦ 850 Get by with a little help from your friends.

If you want to go to the movie theater, try to go with a group of friends and/or colleagues. Most of the major theater chains offer group discounts, typically for groups of ten or more. It's a great way to get everyone together and to save money, too.

### ♦ 851 Use movie discount passes.

Most major movie chains offer discount passes through local employers or when you purchase tickets in blocks of ten or more. Get ahold of one of these passes—you could save up to $3 on the high cost of a movie ticket.

### ◆ 852 Patronize local movie houses.

If you live in a small or medium-size town it may still contain an operating movie house. If you are lucky enough to have one of these establishments in your hometown, catch your movies there. The films that these independent houses show are usually four or five months old, so if you really want to see a brand-new movie, don't expect it to show up on the movie-house screen for a little while. But so what? A good film is just as good three months after it's been released as it is when all the critics are raving about it. You will pay less for your ticket and experience a fast-vanishing piece of Americana in the bargain.

### ◆ 853 If you've just got to own the latest CDs by the Crash Test Dummies, O-Positive, and U-2, buy them all at once.

If you plan to collect a large number of CDs, buy them all at once. Even discount stores offer additional savings on large-quantity purchases.

### ◆ 854 Don't fall prey to book or record clubs that offer you 10 items for a penny if you agree to buy ten more at *their* price.

While some of these clubs really do offer the consumer a good deal, others use fine print to gyp unsuspecting consumers. So before you sign up for anything, do a little math. Add the total price of the items you can buy at the club's special price with the total price of the items you'd be required to buy at the club's regular price. Then divide this number by the total number of items you would acquire. *Don't* sign up if the average per-item cost isn't considerably cheaper than local retailers' prices. Remember those shipping and handling costs!

# 27

# Holidays

In the Middle Ages, peasant villages would elect a "lord of misrule" to preside over, in a raucous impersonation of the local nobleman, the community's Yuletide festivities. Unfortunately, for all too many of us, this merrily anarchic character seems to take charge of our bank accounts every time the holiday season rolls around, making off with a good deal of our hard-earned money in the process.

There's no reason to drain your savings account every holiday season, however. You can enjoy your holidays, throw parties, give gifts, and host feasts but still keep expenses in control. For while he may be good for a few laughs, the lord of misrule doesn't have any business taking over your bank account. This chapter will help your wallet enjoy the holiday season without people calling you a grinch.

## ◆ 855 Cut down on gift-giving.

Don't accuse me of being Ebenezer Scrooge. The plain fact is that most of us spend more on gifts than we should. (The price of a gift is not a measure of affection for our loved ones.) Be more imaginative. Note: You'll know you've got control of your personal finances when you spend at the same rate between Thanksgiving and Christmas as you do between Christmas and Thanksgiving.

## ◆ 856 Buy family members gifts they need.

Sure, it may not be your idea of romance, but if your husband needs a band saw, why not give it to him for his birthday? He's going to enjoy it a lot more than a necktie or a sweater.

241

◆ **857** **Don't go overboard when giving young children holiday gifts.**

Amid the general cacophony and excitement that usually accompany major holidays, individual gifts receive only fleeting attention. Young children have short attention spans, which makes it unlikely that they will lavish much attention on most of their presents.

◆ **858** **Don't buy gifts that require batteries.**

Unless you want to bankrupt the recipient slowly.

◆ **859** **Give gifts that show the recipient the importance of saving.**

Like U.S. savings bonds.

◆ **860** **If you must give an expensive gift, charge it on a credit card that offers "buyer's protection."**

You might as well take advantage of this silly program.

◆ **861** **Don't buy gifts that will keep on costing the recipient money.**

Like the video game gadgets that require cartridges.

◆ **862** **Do your Christmas shopping early, when gifts are on sale.**

Draw up a Christmas shopping game plan well ahead of time. Your efforts will be amply rewarded. Once you know who is getting what, you can purchase gift items when they go on sale. Why fight frenzied last-minute Christmas shoppers for the privilege of paying full price?

◆ **863** **Set some reasonable ground rules regarding gifts for relatives.**

It's easy to lose control when it comes to family gift-giving. If you've always given a gift to your sister, but now she's mar-

ried with children, don't get trapped into giving many gifts.
You'll end up spending a king's ransom on presents. Instead,
suggest to family members that ground rules be set as to who
will receive gifts and who won't. One gift to each family,
rather than one gift to each family member, would be an
appropriate way to keep a financial lid on things.

### ◆ 864   Organize a "secret Santa" at your office.

If holiday gift-giving is getting out of hand at the office,
organize a "secret Santa." Each participant draws out of a
hat a name of a coworker to whom he or she must anony-
mously give one present. Everyone is assured of getting a gift,
and more importantly, each person has to buy only one gift.

### ◆ 865   Make holiday travel plans early.

If you are planning to travel over the holidays, don't delay;
make your travel plans now. If you will be flying, advance
planning could save you a lot of money. Cheap seats go fast.

### ◆ 866   Don't leave home alone.

Driving to Grandma's house for the holidays? Chances are
you can carpool it with like-minded relatives. Share each
other's company, and share the cost of the ride.

### ◆ 867   If you're having guests at your home for the holidays, prepare the food yourself.

Holidays are expensive enough without having to drain the
family coffers by feeding guests. Unless you are hosting a
truly monumental banquet, avoid the expense of a caterer.
Instead, enlist the help of other family members and relatives
who are invariably hanging around during the holidays.

### ◆ 868   Cook it all at once.

If you're preparing the big feast, don't waste time and money
by cooking each item separately. (Cook the roasted potatoes
and the pies together.) Figure out a way to prepare the meal
without being a financial turkey.

## ♦ 869  Ask your guests to bring food and drink if you're having a big holiday banquet.

Victuals aren't cheap and neither are spirits, especially if you plan on feeding a gaggle of revelers. Asking each guest to bring along some food is standard operating procedure these days.

## ♦ 870  Buy an artificial Christmas tree.

This is one argument I lose every Christmas. I'm never told what the natural Christmas tree in our household costs, so I'm sure it's outrageous. Buy an artificial tree and you are bound to save in the long run, unless you grow Christmas trees in your backyard. If you are a purist, however, be sure to buy your natural tree from a local service organization.

## ♦ 871  Make your own wreaths.

Rather than buying a wreath, why not make your own? It's a fun family project, and it saves money.

## ♦ 872  Make your own Christmas tree decorations.

The best Christmas tree decorations are the homemade variety. If there are children about, take advantage of that no-cost source of enthusiastic labor to reduce the expense of adorning your tree.

## ♦ 873  Reuse tinsel.

We use tinsel that has been in the Pond family for generations. It's a New England tradition. While the savings may be small, recycling tinsel sends an important message to the younger generation: Waste is wasteful.

## ♦ 874  Don't spend a fortune in outdoor lighting.

Drive around some neighborhoods during the holiday season and you will think that you're in Las Vegas or Times Square. There must be some sort of no-holds-barred competition among the residents of these neighborhoods. The light shows are stupendous, not to mention gaudy. Someday a jet is going to mistake these Xmas-happy locales for an international airport and attempt to land on some palooka's front lawn. You don't need "a thousand points of light" to celebrate the season, unless you own a large block of stock in your local utility.

## ♦ 875  Get free holiday wrapping paper.

My grandmother taught me this one. Unwrap your holiday presents carefully—the paper you save will be your own (free) holiday wrapping paper for the next festive season.

## ♦ 876  Buy wrapping paper and cards between Christmas and New Year's.

The time to buy holiday wrapping paper and cards is 364 days early. Since paper and cards are more or less standard and change little from year to year, there's no reason why you can't stock up on the old season's leftovers in anticipation of next Christmas. It's too good a deal to pass up.

## ♦ 877  Don't give a thief a gift.

Be extra security-conscious during the holidays. (Burglars just love presents.) Holiday time means your home is most vulnerable to burglars. Buy a $3 timer for lighting at your local hardware store. It could prevent your holiday spirit from being stolen.

# 28

## Travel/Vacations

"**T**raveling is a fool's paradise," wrote Emerson in *Self Reliance*. He could have been describing the typical American tourist, because nine times out of ten, travel transforms the average savings-oriented couple into big spenders. While abroad, ordinarily frugal Americans all too often patronize the best restaurants and shops, spend inordinate sums of money on symphony, theater, and opera seats, and take enough cab rides to make even a New Yorker's head spin. Believe me, it could happen to you.

How can you protect your savings from this variety of temporary insanity? Emerson would have told you to stay home. But if you insist on playing the tourist, however, read this chapter. I'll show you how to get there and back without saying *bon voyage* to your savings.

### ◆ 878  Rent an RV rather than buying one.

Unless you are retired and are going to travel throughout the year, you are probably better off renting a recreational vehicle for your vacations and periodic sojourns rather than buying one. They're an eyesore in your driveway anyway.

### ◆ 879  The same goes for boats.

◆ **880** **If you plan to rent a car overseas, check with your automobile insurer to see if your coverage can be extended to include cars driven overseas.**

If you can avoid having to purchase short-term coverage from the car rental agency, you will most certainly save money. Make sure, however, that your insurer provides you with complete documentation; you don't want to have the rental agency clerk insist that you buy an overpriced policy and find yourself unable to prove the fact that you are indeed already covered.

◆ **881** **Take the train or bus instead of a plane.**

Airlines are continually raising their prices, so consider surface travel. While Amtrak isn't exactly the *Orient Express*, even in America you may find traveling by rail a sensible alternative to flying. In Europe, of course, rail service is almost always superior. When you add the time it takes to get to and from the airport, surface travel for shorter distances becomes even more appealing. Unlike airports, train and bus terminals are almost always located in cities' hearts. Not only will you save money, you'll also be able to enjoy a seat that, unlike an airplane seat, is more than six inches wide.

◆ **882** **Make your airline reservations well in advance.**

The cheapest airfares go fast, so plan ahead and make your reservations as soon as your plans are firm.

◆ **883** **Stay over a Saturday night on airline trips.**

Airfares are generally much cheaper if you stay over a Saturday night. The extra night in a hotel is usually a fraction of the airfare savings.

◆ **884** **Travel with cheap luggage.**

Unless you travel by private jet, your luggage is subject to cruel and unusual punishment every time you entrust it to an airline or other transportation company. The airlines also lose about 150,000 pieces of luggage each month. So in addition to traveling cheap, travel with cheap luggage.

♦ **885**   **Rather than hail a cab, take a bus or subway to and from the airport.**

Most airports are accessible via mass transit, so rather than taking a cab or renting a car, you could probably save some money by "taking the A train." If you are unfamiliar with your destination's mass transit system, your travel agent should be able to help.

♦ **886**   **Share cabs to or from the airport or train station.**

If you're in a cab queue, you are probably in line with some people who would love to share the cost of a cab with you. Don't be shy about asking.

♦ **887**   **Ask a relative or friend to drive you to or from the airport.**

The price is right.

♦ **888**   **If you can wait until the last minute, check with travel discounters.**

The airlines, air charter companies, and cruise lines would rather fill a seat or berth for a song than have it remain empty. Several travel agencies specialize in this deeply discounted travel. If time is on your side, it's time to check them out.

♦ **889**   **Fly standby.**

If you've got the time, flying standby can result in big savings.

♦ **890**   **Give up your seat if your flight is overbooked.**

Airlines regularly overbook flights, so they often ask for volunteers to give up their seats. If you can spare the time, you will get to your destination on the next available flight, and you'll be amply rewarded—typically with a round-trip ticket anywhere the airline flies.

♦ **891** **Use a pay phone to make calls rather than pay the hotel fee for the privilege of making a call from your room.**

All you have to do is stroll down to the lobby to make your calls: You will save money (if you have a telephone credit card) by avoiding hotel phone service charges and get some exercise in the process. In fact, some hotel managements charge guests for using the in-room phone even if the call doesn't go through. Outrageous!

♦ **892** **Go out to get your meals rather than getting room service at the hotel.**

At a New York hotel where I stay when someone else is picking up the tab, a Continental breakfast costs $18!! I can walk a half block and get the same combination of orange juice, muffin, and coffee for about $2. So as soon as you check into your hostelry, check out the immediate neighborhood to find some good, affordable eateries.

♦ **893** **Seek out offbeat restaurants favored by locals rather than those catering to tourists.**

If you really want to enjoy the flavor of a city or resort area, ask the locals where they go out to eat. The last places they would probably mention are tourist restaurants, establishments offering mediocre fare at high prices.

♦ **894** **Never use the hotel in-room minibar.**

I would rather expire from thirst than pay absurdly high prices for pathetically small bottles of aqua vitae.

### ◆ 895  Take snacks on a flight.

I recently took a five-hour flight during which I was fed only a sandwich so small that I didn't even need to chew it. When I finally hit the ground, I hit it running: I was so famished that I ran right to the airport snack bar and gladly paid $4 for a soggy hot dog. Next time I'll bring along a snack box, and you should too. Some of my friends concoct truly gourmet travel snacks and go so far as to claim that these delicacies make flying enjoyable.

### ◆ 896  Join frequent-flier programs.

You have nothing to lose by joining an airline's frequent-flier program. You never know—you might accumulate enough mileage to qualify for a free flight or some other freebie.

### ◆ 897  Take a good-cause vacation.

A growing number of environmental, religious, and other groups are sponsoring trips that combine vacation with good works. You can see interesting parts of the world at low cost while also doing the world some good.

### ◆ 898  Save on housing with elder/youth hostels.

Elder hostels, youth hostels, and everyone hostels offer inexpensive housing and the opportunity to meet interesting people throughout the world.

### ◆ 899  Tap your alumni organization for good housing deals.

Many college alumni organizations have reciprocal arrangements with other alumni associations to offer low-cost housing in many locales. Educate yourself on any programs offered by your alma mater.

### ◆ 900  Stay in a college dorm—cheap.

Numerous colleges provide cheap housing in their dormitories during college vacation periods.

**♦ 901    Combine pleasure trips with business trips.**

If a business trip takes you to a location that you and, perhaps, your family might enjoy, consider combining pleasure with business. Since airlines often provide deeply discounted fares for trips on which one stays over a Saturday night, your spending an extra couple of days or more at a location enjoying the sights might be a money-saver.

**♦ 902    Avoid making purchases in tourist/vacation areas.**

Souvenirs are wonderful, but you can probably buy the T-shirt or whatever for a lot less if you find a store that is not in the midst of a tourist/vacation mecca. The same can be said for other items you may want to purchase during your vacation.

**♦ 903    Inquire about discounts when making hotel/motel reservations.**

You have to ask, because the reservations agents aren't going to be forthcoming with the information. But often discounts on room rates are available for employees of certain companies, members of certain organizations, certain age groups, weekend stays, etc., etc. Be sure to ask.

**♦ 904    Take your luggage into the terminal to check it rather than use curbside check-in.**

Unless your luggage is incredibly heavy or your plane is just about to taxi down the runway, carry your bags into the terminal so you won't need to tip the curbside check-in personnel. It may save only a small amount of money, but it's your money, right?

**♦ 905    Plan your vacation so you can take advantage of hotel/motel and other travel discounts.**

If you are planning a vacation, find out whether you might be eligible for various discounts. You may be eligible for discounts depending upon where you travel, the time you travel, and the duration of your stay. Don't pass up valuable discounts through poor travel planning.

### ◆ 906 Obtain airfare quotations from two or three sources, including the airline itself.

The airfare system is a mess, and the consumer is at its mercy. The only way to make sure you are getting a good fare is to check several different sources. You'll be amazed in the differences in the rates you are quoted, but by comparison shopping you will be able to buy your ticket with some confidence that you are getting a good deal.

### ◆ 907 Never buy anything in an airport gift shop.

With the exception of newspapers, magazines, and books, avoid buying anything at an airport gift shop. If you want to bestow gifts on family members, the only thing you can be sure of about what you buy in an airport gift shop is that you are paying top dollar.

### ◆ 908 Never buy anything in a hotel gift shop.

See the above comments on airport gift shops. They are equally applicable to hotel gift shops.

### ◆ 909 Register early.

If you are attending a conference or meeting, whether it is for business or pleasure, register early if the sponsor offers a discount for early registrants. In fact, the earlier you plan the details of your travel, the more money you are likely to save.

### ◆ 910 Take home any goodies that you don't use up in your hotel/motel room.

The hotel and motel chains seem to be engaging in a no-holds-barred competition over the number of "amenities"—shampoo, imported soap, sewing kits—that they can provide their guests. You'd be crazy to buy these overpriced fripperies on your own. Well, if you've used some of these items, be sure to take home the unused portions. They will work just as well in your own bathroom as they did in the hotel.

## ◆ 911 If you're driving a long distance, take someone along to share the expenses.

If you are going on an automobile trip, find someone who needs to go to the same destination. He or she can split expenses with you. Or vice versa.

## ◆ 912 If you're buying bargains overseas, be sure to consider the customs duty.

Many overseas travelers have a rude awakening when they find out how much in customs duties they will have to pay for purchases made overseas. When you are facing a revenue-hungry customs officer, these items won't seem like such a bargain. So be sure to factor in the effect of customs duties when you shop overseas.

## ◆ 913 Before traveling overseas, check the local price of any items you intend to purchase during your sojourn abroad.

What may seem like a bargain when you are several thousand miles from home and basking in some romantic clime may actually have cost significantly less had you purchased it Stateside. Therefore, if you plan to make an expensive purchase overseas, check on what it costs locally before you make your trip so you'll know whether you are truly getting a bargain.

## ◆ 914 Join hotel/motel frequent-guest programs.

Just like the airlines, hotels and motels want to build up and reward a loyal clientele. If you travel more than sporadically, join hotel/motel frequent-guest programs. Who knows? You might get some free lodging.

### ♦ 915 Four nights might get you one or more nights free.

If you're going to stay at a hotel or motel for several nights, find out if they offer a free night or nights for guests on an extended trip.

### ♦ 916 Consider trip cancellation insurance.

If you foresee the possibility that a prepaid vacation may have to be canceled, purchasing trip cancellation insurance may end up saving you a lot of money.

### ♦ 917 You don't have to go on a tour to get travel bargains.

While group travel tours are a very economical way to travel, many people don't want to travel in a herd. If you are a rugged individualist, look for travel packages that offer "tour rates" but don't oblige you to spend your vacation listening to some shower curtain ring salesman tell you about his kids.

### ♦ 918 Go to resorts in the off-season.

If you play your cards right, you can visit a resort just before the season rates begin or just after they end. You might enjoy a less-crowded resort when you visit in the off-season, and you'll certainly enjoy the money you save.

### ♦ 919 Use campgrounds rather than hotels for vacations.

You can save a lot of money when you "rough it" instead of staying at a hotel or resort, and you'll be healthier for it.

### ♦ 920 Take vacations closer to home or at home.

There are probably great places to vacation near or in your hometown. Many people live close to vacation areas that other people travel hundreds or thousands of miles to visit. And think about the number of sights right around your home that you have yet to see. Vacation near or at home this year!

## ♦ 921   Stay at budget hotels and motels.

There is a lot of difference in the cost of a typical luxury hotel or motel and the rapidly growing cadre of budget hostelries. Most people who have stayed in lower-cost lodgings swear by them—that's why budget hotels and motels are thriving in the midst of a flat economy. Remember, when you go on vacation, you generally spend so little time in your room that you don't really need antique furniture or an entertainment center.

## ♦ 922   Rent a condo or vacation cottage rather than staying in a hotel.

If you are planning to vacation in an area that has condos, vacation cottages, or other types of rental accommodation, compare their prices with those of local hotels or inns. You may find—especially if you have a large brood or group of friends with you—that renting a cottage or house is a very economical solution. Shop around for the best price, however, and be prepared to haggle with the renter—many resort areas are suffering from overbuilding, and rates are quite competitive. I've known some people who have vacationed for the past five years in Florida and have watched the rental rates for their condo decline with each passing year.

## ♦ 923   Stay with friends or relatives.

Cut way down on vacation costs by staying with relatives or friends. If they reside near a popular vacation destination, they are probably used to having people stay over.

## ♦ 924   Negotiate hotel room rates.

While some people are good hagglers, others are hesitant to plunge into the give-and-take of serious bargaining. Don't let yourself be intimidated: Like the sale price of a house, the rental rate on a hotel or motel room is eminently negotiable.

## ♦ 925   Double-check your hotel/motel bill.

Don't just blithely accept your hotel or motel bill when you check out. Double-check it out for errors.

## ◆ 926 Make sure you are adequately insured if you are traveling abroad.

Before you take a trip overseas, check that your insurance coverage, particularly medical insurance, includes overseas travel. Most policies are effective in foreign countries, but double-check anyway. You don't want to get appendicitis in Azerbaijan and find out that you have to pay the hospital in cash before the doctors will operate. Senior citizens take note: Medicare provides almost no coverage outside the United States and its territories. Ask your travel agent or travel organization about obtaining supplementary insurance for your trip.

## ◆ 927 Don't buy a yearly airline pass unless you are going to use it often enough to justify the cost.

Sometimes what initially seems to be a great purchase ends up becoming a costly mistake. Yearly airline passes can be attractive to people who can make good use of them. Don't buy one, however, until you have carefully planned your itinerary so that planned travel is sufficient to justify the cost of the ticket.

## ◆ 928 Check into fly-drive packages that combine airfares with accommodations and car rentals.

The airlines are in cahoots with the rental car agencies, and you can benefit from this situation. Fly-drive packages can combine discounted airfares with discounted car rentals. If you are going to need to rent a car when you reach your destination, be sure to investigate some of these convenient packages.

## ◆ 929 Bed-and-breakfast it—try it, you'll like it.

Some people turn up their noses at bed-and-breakfast establishments, but the better B-and-Bs are inheritors of the best traditions of the old-fashioned inn. They range in size and luxury from places that consist of a couple of spare rooms in a private home to luxurious establishments that differ from hotels only in their lack of a restaurant. Many B-and-Bs are in restored eighteenth- or nineteenth-century houses and have great historic character. Bed-and-breakfasts have a great deal more charm and personality than most hotels, and their prices have a good deal of charm, too.

### ◆ 930 Find someone to travel with you.

If you are single, you probably realize that traveling alone costs a great deal more on a per-person basis than does traveling with a companion. This is especially true with accommodations, so if you have a friend who is willing to split your planned trip's expenses with you, convince him or her to come along.

### ◆ 931 When making purchases abroad, find out how to avoid paying local taxes.

If you think that sales taxes are bad in your home state, you will be horrified by the taxes that foreign countries levy on *their* consumers. In many cases, however, these countries— well aware of the importance of tourist dollars—have established methods to reimburse travelers for domestic taxes such as the infamous value-added-tax (VAT).

### ◆ 932 Interrupt newspaper service if you're going to be away from home for an extended period.

If you're going to be on vacation or on an extended business trip, save money and, perhaps, avoid a burglary by having your newspaper delivery service interrupted until you get back.

### ◆ 933 Let neighbors know when you're going to be traveling.

One of the best deterrents against burglary is a vigilant neighbor. Be sure to let your neighbors know when and how long you'll be gone. It just may prevent an unwanted and expensive interruption of your travels.

# IX

# LATER
# LIFE

# 29

# Senior Citizens

It used to be that senior citizens were revered by their families and their communities. Then we went through a period when being elderly was a curse. Now, thank heavens, the pendulum is swinging back to where it rightfully belongs—and should remain. Cutting back on living expenses is often a particular concern to retired people because of the triple whammy of inflation, fixed incomes, and (hopefully) longer retirements.

The following suggestions will help you take maximum advantage of the many discounts and benefits available to senior citizens. Other techniques that many seniors employ to reduce their living expenses, sometimes dramatically, are also presented.

### ◆ 934  Join the AARP and other organizations that promote the interests of senior citizens.

It doesn't cost much to join the AARP ($5) and other senior citizen organizations. If you participate in the programs and discounts they offer, your return on such a small investment will be spectacular.

### ◆ 935  Plan now to avoid falling behind to inflation.

One of the biggest fears (and problems) of senior citizens is falling behind to inflation. Since the income of many retired people is fixed or doesn't keep pace with inflation, they risk falling farther and farther behind in meeting ever-increasing living costs. What this means for most retirees is that they will have to continue saving during the first ten years or so of their retirement so they will have more money available in later years to keep up with inflation. What's most important is to make projections of income and living expenses and devise a plan today that will allow you to enjoy retirement for the rest of your life. It may require some cutting back now, but that is far preferable to having to make drastic cutbacks later.

### ♦ 936 Take advantage of special banking programs for senior citizens.

Numerous banks offer special banking programs for older customers, including discounts on checking account fees. But you have to let the bank know that you qualify. Wouldn't it be nice if the banks started to give free money to seniors?

### ♦ 937 Check with your state agency on aging for information on state and federal programs for seniors.

Each state has an agency that acts as a clearinghouse for information on state and federal programs for older Americans. Contact your state's senior citizens agency to find out about what state programs are available to you. They could be money-savers.

### ♦ 938 Use direct deposit for your Social Security check.

Get your money faster and safer by asking Social Security to deposit your check directly into your checking account.

### ♦ 939 Don't borrow against your house if you think you might enter a nursing home.

In the event that you have to enter a nursing home and "spend down" until you qualify for Medicaid, one of the few assets that you can protect is the equity in your home. If however, you borrow against that equity, the money you get from the loan will probably have to go toward meeting your health care costs. Rules pertaining to qualifying for Medicaid vary and are subject to change, so be sure to check on the particulars with someone in the know.

## ♦ 940 Plan trips and vacations through senior citizen organizations.

Many senior citizen organizations sponsor low-cost day and weekend trips and longer vacations. If you like a bargain, check these organizations out.

## ♦ 941 To the extent possible, travel at off-peak seasons, days of the week, and times of day.

Retired people usually have a lot more flexibility in making travel plans—whether they are traveling across town or across the country. Save wear and tear on yourself and, often, your wallet by traveling at off-peak seasons, days of the week, and times of day.

## ♦ 942 Always ask for senior citizen discounts at hotels, motels, and travel agencies.

Senior citizen discounts abound as more and more people enter their golden years. Get into the habit of always inquiring about senior citizen discounts. You'll like what you hear.

## ♦ 943 When buying pharmaceuticals, whenever possible use drugstores that offer senior citizen discounts.

Many drugstores are jumping on the senior citizen discount bandwagon. Hop on.

## ♦ 944 Consider bulk purchases of prescription drugs you use repetitively.

Prescription drugs cost a small fortune these days. If you use some repetitively, be sure to comparison-shop on the rates for bulk purchases offered by the AARP as well as other firms that offer prescription drugs by mail.

### ◆ 945   Let your hair "go natural."

Why go to the expense of hiding the natural color of your locks? It's cool to let your hair go natural.

### ◆ 946   Evaluate your driving habits.

Do you really need a car? Many seniors use their car so little that they could actually save money by getting rid of their car and taking cabs or public transit whenever they need "wheels."

### ◆ 947   Match the cost of an item to its expected useful life.

Don't go to the expense of buying a long-lasting product if you don't expect to use it over the product's entire expected useful life. For example, an elderly person who doesn't expect to remain in his or her home for many more years need not spend thousands of dollars on heirloom-quality dining-room furniture. Less expensive furniture would probably suffice.

### ◆ 948   Consider the way you use an item. Gentle, less rigorous use may suggest a cheaper purchase.

If you don't make heavy use of an item, you can probably get by with a less durable, less expensive product.

### ◆ 949   Share maintenance service with neighbors.

Many seniors who live in the same neighborhood get together to coordinate work that needs to be done in several households so they can obtain a discount from local tradespeople for a multihousehold deal. It's a win-win situation.

### ◆ 950   Downscale your food purchases.

Many older people continue to shop for groceries as if they still had a brood of hungry kids around the house. Don't buy a lot of food you probably won't consume.

### ◆ 951 Bulk purchases won't save money if unused portions are discarded.

While bulk purchases of food are fine if you have a lot of mouths to feed, empty-nesters should generally avoid buying in bulk if unused portions are likely to languish on their shelves and end up being discarded.

### ◆ 952 Consider possible financial advantages of "downsizing" living accommodations.

I'm amazed at the number of senior citizens who insist on staying in the large home that, typically, they raised their family in. They don't really need all that space, upkeep is a burden, and the cost of maintaining a larger-than-necessary home can put a big dent in a retirement nest egg. If you are living in a large home and are already retired or nearing retirement, consider the many advantages, financial and otherwise, of downsizing your living accommodations.

### ◆ 953 Investigate the variety of housing options available for seniors.

Housing is both a big concern and a big expense for older people, particularly those who are renters and, therefore, always subject to rent increases. Whatever your housing situation, investigate the many housing options available to senior citizens. Chances are there is a housing arrangement that will meet both your financial requirements and life-style preferences, but like all good things, it takes some digging.

### ◆ 954 Sell your house to your children.

You may be able to reduce your living expenses, stay in your home forever, yet still tap into the equity in your home by selling it to your children.

### ◆ 955 Take advantage of property tax and/or rent breaks that may be available to senior citizens.

Many communities are giving tax and/or rent concessions to senior citizens. Find out if some might apply to you.

### ♦ 956 Take advantage of restaurants/movies/ barbers and beauty salons/stores that offer senior discounts.

So many businesses are offering discounts to senior citizens that younger people can't wait to reach age sixty-five so they can begin enjoying the savings. Whoever said getting old was no fun obviously didn't know about senior citizen discounts. Be sure to ask your friends about any senior citizen discounts *they* have found.

### ♦ 957 Get a senior citizen transit pass.

Don't pass up the savings of a senior citizen transit pass if you qualify. Why pay full price if you don't have to?

### ♦ 958 Take advantage of educational program discounts for seniors.

Many local schools and colleges give discounts to senior citizens for their continuing education programs. It's a great way to keep on learning at a very reasonable cost.

### ♦ 959 Prepare a list of stores and organizations that offer senior citizen discounts.

The best way to make sure you take as much advantage as possible of discounts for senior citizens is to prepare and keep up-to-date a list of stores and organizations that offer senior citizen discounts. Otherwise it's too easy to forget who offers what discounts. Be sure to share your list with your friends.

### ♦ 960 Always be wary of charlatans who prey on senior citizens.

Sadly, seniors are often victimized by unscrupulous individuals who sell them things they don't need or things they may need at vastly inflated prices. Either way, you end up losing money. Always be on the lookout for these scalawags, and if you ever have the slightest doubt, don't buy anything until you have checked them out.

## ♦ 961  Check with your children or close friends before making any major financial commitment.

Whenever you are contemplating making a major financial decision—a change in housing, a home improvement, a new insurance policy, a new investment—be sure to check out your plans with your children or close friends. It's always useful to get a second (or third) opinion on important financial matters.

# 30

## Estate Taxes

**M**ost people think they don't have enough money to be concerned about estate taxes, but many of them are wrong. Even though you may not have much in the way of assets now, you may in the future. Therefore it behooves you at least to consider techniques you can employ to reduce your estate taxes. While most planning strategies end up saving money only after your demise, some may actually provide tax savings during your lifetime.

### ◆ 962 If you have a large estate and can afford it, take advantage of the annual gift exclusion to transfer assets to children and grandchildren.

You can reduce the size of your taxable estate by giving as much as $10,000 away per donee per donor. In other words, you and your spouse could give as much as $20,000 per year to each of your children and grandchildren. Of course, they will love to receive the money, but be sure you don't give away more money than you can comfortably afford.

### ♦ 963 Consult with an attorney about taking advantage of using your unified credit during your lifetime.

Some people who are blessed with a lot of money are often advised by estate-planning lawyers to make transfers of up to the $600,000 unified credit to their children or grandchildren during their lifetime rather than deferring the credit until the estate is eventually settled.

### ♦ 964 A unified credit trust can increase the amount of money your heirs will inherit.

The estate-tax savings can be dramatic, although you won't live to see them. If you are married and your estate is likely to exceed $600,000 in value, consult your attorney about establishing a unified credit trust under the terms of your will. On the death of you and your spouse, the heirs will save as much as $235,000 in estate taxes by having the language necessary to establish this straightforward trust established in both your and your spouse's wills.

### ♦ 965 Transferring assets to irrevocable trusts during your life can reduce estate taxes.

Irrevocable trusts have a variety of advantages, including the ability to reduce the taxes that would eventually be levied on your estate. However, as the name suggests, these transfers can't be undone, so they require a great deal of thought on your part.

### ♦ 966 Consider putting your life-insurance policy into a life-insurance trust.

Taking this action could result in dramatic estate-tax savings for your heirs. When you simply name beneficiaries to your life-insurance policy, the policy's proceeds are includable in your estate for tax purposes. But if you think your—or your spouse's—estate will be sufficiently large to be subject to these taxes, consider transferring your life-insurance policy into a so-called life-insurance trust.

◆ **967** **Transfer an unneeded life-insurance policy to a charity.**

If you have a life-insurance policy that your heirs don't need, consider naming a charity as its beneficiary. In that way your estate won't have to pay taxes on the death benefits. You'll get a charitable deduction for the donation and possibly other benefits as well.

◆ **968** **Check with your lawyer to see if there is any action you should take to minimize state death taxes.**

Just as there are ways to reduce, if not eliminate, federal estate taxes, so state death tax saving opportunities may be available in your home state. Ask your estate planning attorney to review your situation and suggest any actions that should be taken to minimize state death taxes.

◆ **969** **Move to a state that has lower state death taxes.**

The death tax that a state can assess varies dramatically from state to state. You can save your heirs a considerable amount of money by moving to a state that levies low state death taxes.

◆ **970** **Consider a private annuity with your children.**

Private annuities are arrangements, usually with family members, that typically involve the parents transferring their home to their children in exchange for a lifetime annuity. The parents can reside in the home, pay rent to the children, get annuity payments back from the children, defer income taxes, and save on estate taxes. Whew!

◆ **971** **Owning real estate or property in more than one state can be costly.**

Maintaining houses or other property in several states is a time-consuming business in itself. Upon death, however, multistate property ownership can be an estate-tax nightmare. Why? Because each state in which you owned property may well try to grab a piece of the action by levying death taxes on your estate. So whether your domain stretches across state boundaries or consists of scattered holdings in several states, ask your attorney about appropriate strategies. Placing properties into a living trust may help protect your estate from revenue-hungry state governments.

♦ **972**   **If you have homes in more than one state, establish residence in the state with the lower state death tax rates.**

Your heirs will appreciate your foresight. An attorney can guide you in what is necessary to establish residence in a particular state.

♦ **973**   **Don't designate yourself as custodian for a child's investment account.**

While it may be customary and convenient to name yourself as custodian when you give money to your kids, this could backfire since the IRS may still include those assets in your taxable estate if you die before your child becomes age eighteen or twenty-one.

♦ **974**   **Pay college tuition for grandchildren directly to the college.**

In estate-planning parlance, there is an unlimited gift tax exclusion for qualifying payments of tuition. In plain English this means that, in addition to the $10,000 annual gift exclusion, you are permitted to make tuition payments on behalf of grandchildren (or anyone else, for that matter) without running afoul of the gift- and estate-tax rules. Be sure to make these payments directly to the educational institution so there is no question about how the money was used.

♦ **975**   **If you pay medical expenses on behalf of your parents, make payments directly to the health care provider.**

The above-mentioned point with respect to college tuition payments also applies to the payment of medical expenses as long as they are not reimbursed by insurance. The medical expense exclusion may be of particular value in providing care for an aged parent.

### ◆ 976 Investigate ways to transfer your family business to younger family members to reduce your estate-tax liability.

While Congress has tightened the rules on passing on family businesses to children, there are still opportunities to make a transfer while minimizing estate taxes. What is required? A lot of planning in consultation with an expert in these matters.

### ◆ 977 Use of the alternate valuation date may reduce estate taxes.

The executor of an estate may elect to have estate assets valued at the date of death or on an alternate date six months later. If the value of the estate is declining, perhaps due to soft stock or real-estate prices, using the alternate valuation date will save estate taxes.

### ◆ 978 Don't delay if you are planning to utilize sophisticated estate-planning techniques.

Of course it's unpleasant dealing with estate-planning matters because they remind us of our own mortality. But there may be good reason not to tarry, beyond the obvious one that we never know when the Grim Reaper will come calling. The U.S. Congress has been threatening over the past few years to curtail many of the estate-tax saving benefits available to people with large estates. Someday they will make good on this threat, although it is very unlikely that the more restrictive rules will apply to those estate plans and trusts that have already been implemented. So don't waste time.

# 31

## YOUR ESTATE

**W**e've come to the end of the line. While most of us don't want to contemplate our mortality, death and taxes are the only two certainties in life. (At least death, unlike taxes, doesn't get worse every time Congress convenes.) There are a variety of things you can do in planning your estate that will not only make life easier for your loved ones after you're gone but also can save them a lot of unnecessary expense. Perhaps this is an important legacy to pass on to the younger generation.

### ◆ 979  Prepare a will.

Unless you detest your heirs and want to curse them with a terrible legal mess, prepare a will. Otherwise your heirs will have to spend a lot of time and money administering your estate, a situation that is easily avoided by properly preparing a will.

### ◆ 980  Periodically check that your will is valid and up-to-date.

Just because you have a will doesn't mean it is still valid. Family relationships change, people relocate to another state, and state and federal laws change. The only positive thing that can be said about dying with an invalid will is that you won't be around to witness the expensive problems it can cause.

### ◆ 981  Don't have a joint will.

While joint wills may sound lovey-dovey, they can cause a lot of problems. These wills offer great opportunities for expensive legal disputes and other costly problems. It doesn't cost a lot to have separate wills prepared, and, in the long run, it can save a lot of time, money, and hassle.

### ◆ 982  Appoint a family member as executor of your estate.

Rather than paying an outsider to be executor of your estate, appoint a capable family member instead. Your heirs should end up saving money, even if the family member needs outside help to administer your estate.

### ◆ 983  Appoint a capable guardian for your minor children.

Nineteenth-century novels are replete with wicked uncles who mistreat their orphaned relatives, and despite the melodrama, these stories contain a grain of truth. So don't take the task of designating a guardian for your children lightly. Appointing people who are not up to the task could be an expensive mistake.

### ◆ 984  Prepare a durable power of attorney.

A durable power of attorney is another important estate-planning document that designates someone to take care of you in the event you become incapacitated. Without this document the courts would have to appoint a guardian for you. Because a court of law was never intended to deal with this sort of situation, having a judge appoint a guardian could be a costly, time-consuming, and acrimonious proceeding.

### ◆ 985  Don't necessarily believe that living trusts are essential to your estate planning.

Living trusts are a hot topic these days, and some people would have you believe that they are essential to your estate planning. While living trusts can provide many important benefits to individuals and couples, they are vastly oversold. So before going to the expense of having a living trust prepared, take a hard look at what it can and cannot do for you.

### ♦ 986 Trying to avoid probate at all costs can be costly.

A lot of people think that probate is a dirty word and will spend a great deal of money structuring their estates to avoid it. Unfortunately, they end up spending more on probate avoidance than they would have spent had the estate gone through probate.

### ♦ 987 Prepare a living will.

Most people want to have a living will, which specifies that extraordinary measures not be taken to keep a terminally ill person alive. This can be a very costly oversight, both emotionally and financially, particularly if the family has to spend a considerable amount of money sustaining your life.

### ♦ 988 Prepare a letter of instructions.

This document informs family members about important matters that need to be settled after your death. It includes details about your personal finances. A well-prepared letter of instructions will save your loved ones a lot of time—and expense—in organizing and administering your estate.

### ♦ 989 Talk to your favorite charity about charitable remainder trusts, charitable gift annuities, and pooled-income funds.

It would take another book to explain these charitable giving strategies. Suffice it to say, however, if you are charitably inclined, you may be able to have your cake and eat it, too. For example, charitable remainder trusts allow you to enjoy the income produced by a charitable gift of cash or investments—which is thus removed from your estate, lowering your estate-tax exposure—while getting a partial tax deduction at the time the trust is established. Upon your death, the principal is then given directly to the charity. Your charity will be happy to explain these marvelous programs to you.

### ♦ 990 GRITs may be good for your heirs' financial health.

GRITs and other similar estate-planning tools are designed to reduce your estate-tax liability while allowing you still to earn some income on the trust assets. If this sounds complicated, that's because it is, so seek the advice of an estate-planning attorney. By the way, a GRIT is a grantor-retained income trust.

### ♦ 991 Set up a sprinkling trust to shift income to lower-tax-bracket family members.

A sprinkling (or "spraying") trust empowers a trustee to give varying levels of income to beneficiaries. It can be used to shift income to those family members who are in a lower tax bracket, thereby lowering the total family tax burden.

### ♦ 992 Die holding a lot of unrealized capital gains.

This may be a high price to pay, but if you die holding real estate and investments that have appreciated substantially in value, your estate and your heirs may avoid paying capital gains on those securities, since their value is "stepped up" to the market value as of the date of death. If it sounds a little complicated, it can be. Still, you should check it out with your lawyer or accountant.

### ♦ 993 Medical expenses paid within one year after death are deductible in the year incurred.

Unfortunately, you have to die to reap the benefits of post-death medical payments. The rules are complicated, but it's wise to say that there may be either income-tax or estate-tax benefits to medical expenses paid after death. If you happen to be the executor of a loved one's estate, pay special attention to the rules, since they could end up saving the heirs money.

## ◆ 994 Make your funeral wishes known.

Tell your relatives exactly how you want your funeral handled. Better yet, include these details as part of your will. By making your wishes clear, you will save your survivors the pain of agonizing over these details at such a distressing time.

## ◆ 995 Ask for a modest funeral.

One of the best ways to encourage your family not to go broke with a lavish funeral is to describe in writing the kind of modest funeral or memorial service you want. The more detailed the instructions, the more likely they will conform to your wishes.

## ◆ 996 Pay for your funeral today.

Perhaps the best way to ensure that your funeral costs are kept under control is to prepay your funeral. Most funeral homes offer prepayment plans.

## ◆ 997 Buy a family burial plot.

You have heard of economies of scale. You can take advantage of this basic rule of economics by purchasing one large burial plot instead of several individual ones. In that way you can divide up the plot's cost among all its future residents.

## ◆ 998 Share a burial plot.

Check to see if you can be buried on top of another family member—two for the price of one.

## ◆ 999 Ask for a modest tombstone.

However you plan for your funeral, don't forget to ask for a modest tombstone or marker. I think you'll agree that there is no need to adorn your final resting place with a twenty-foot-tall Carrara marble obelisk or a poured-concrete replica of the Pietà. Come to think of it, who could rest with all that weight pressing down on them anyway?

## ◆ **1000** Donate your remains to science.

You can help advance scientific knowledge while reducing what are euphemistically called "final disposition costs" if you donate your remains to a medical school.

## ◆ **1001** Ask to be cremated.

This is the end, number 1001. While you won't enjoy any benefits from this expense-saving tactic, your heirs will.

# X

# PUTTING SAVINGS INTO ACTION

# 32

## Start Cutting Expenses Now

**N**ow that you've reviewed the 1001 ways and hopefully found a number that you can apply to your life, it's time to get organized, set goals for yourself, and put these cost-cutting measures into effect.

### Personal Savings Planner

The following work sheet can be used to plan your own personal savings program in four steps.

*First,* write down how much you would like to reduce your expenses each month.

*Second,* note which of the 1001 ways to cut your expenses you are going to use.

*Third,* estimate the monthly savings you will earn for each item.

*Fourth,* keep adding items until the total monthly savings equal or exceed your desired reduction in expenses.

## Personal Savings Worksheet

I would like to reduce my monthly expenses by $_____.

I will reduce my expenses by taking the following steps:

| Description | Estimated Monthly Savings |
|---|---|
| | $_____ |
| | _____ |
| | _____ |
| | _____ |
| | _____ |
| | _____ |
| | _____ |
| | _____ |
| *Total estimated monthly savings* | $_____ |

## Monthly Expense Budget

Use the following monthly expense budget to plan how much you expect to spend over a particular month and then to compare the amounts actually spent against the amounts you budgeted.

### For the Month of _____ 19____

| | Amount Budgeted | Amount Spent |
|---|---|---|
| Food | $_____ | $_____ |
| Housing | _____ | _____ |
| Insurance | _____ | _____ |
| Clothing | _____ | _____ |
| Transportation | _____ | _____ |
| Medical and dental care | _____ | _____ |
| Personal care | _____ | _____ |
| Tuition/educational expenses | _____ | _____ |
| Entertainment | _____ | _____ |
| Contributions | _____ | _____ |
| Gifts | _____ | _____ |
| Laundry and dry cleaning | _____ | _____ |
| Childcare | _____ | _____ |
| Other: | _____ | _____ |
| _____ | _____ | _____ |
| _____ | _____ | _____ |
| *Total* | $_____ | $_____ |

## Personal Budget Planner

One of the best ways to get a handle on how you spend your money is to prepare a personal budget, just like businesses prepare budgets. This work sheet can be used either to record your past cash receipts and cash disbursements and/or to budget future receipts and disbursements. You may want to use the first column to record your past receipts and disbursements; the second column to list your budget over the next month, quarter, or year; and the third column to compare your actual future receipts and disbursements against your budget in the second column. If you budget over a period of less than one year, be sure to take into consideration those expenses that you pay less frequently than monthly, such as insurance, vacations, and tuition. You should be setting aside an amount each month that will eventually cover those large bills.

Indicate at the top of each column whether the amounts in that column are actual or estimated past figures or budgeted future figures. Also indicate the time period in each column (e.g., "January 1993" or "Year 1994").

Indicate if actual or
budget:                          _____      _____      _____

Indicate the time period:        _____      _____      _____

### Cash Receipts

Gross salary                  $_____    $_____    $_____

Interest                         _____      _____      _____

Dividends                        _____      _____      _____

Bonuses/profit sharing           _____      _____      _____

Alimony/child support
  received                       _____      _____      _____

Distributions from
  partnerships                   _____      _____      _____

Income from outside
  business                       _____      _____      _____

| | | | |
|---|---|---|---|
| Trust distributions | | | |
| Pension | | | |
| Social Security | | | |
| Gifts | | | |
| Proceeds from sale of investments | | | |
| Other: | | | |
| | | | |
| | | | |
| | | | |
| *Total cash receipts* | $ | $ | $ |

**Cash Disbursements**

| | | | |
|---|---|---|---|
| Housing (rent/mortgage) | $ | $ | $ |
| Food | | | |
| Household maintenance | | | |
| Utilities and telephone | | | |
| Clothing | | | |
| Personal care | | | |
| Medical and dental care | | | |
| Automobile/ transportation | | | |
| Childcare expenses | | | |
| Entertainment | | | |
| Vacation or vacations | | | |
| Gifts | | | |
| Contributions | | | |

Insurance _____ _____ _____

Miscellaneous out-of-
pocket expenses _____ _____ _____

Furniture _____ _____ _____

Home improvements _____ _____ _____

Real-estate taxes _____ _____ _____

Loan payments _____ _____ _____

Credit card payments _____ _____ _____

Alimony/child support
payments _____ _____ _____

Tuition/educational
expenses _____ _____ _____

Business and professional
expenses _____ _____ _____

Savings/investments _____ _____ _____

Income and Social
Security taxes _____ _____ _____

Other:

_____ _____ _____ _____

_____ _____ _____ _____

*Total cash disbursements* $_____ $_____ $_____

*Excess (shortfall) of cash
receipts over cash
disbursements* $_____ $_____ $_____

## THE HALL OF FAME:
## The Twenty-five Best Things to Do with Your Money

As you can see from the preceding chapters, there are so many ways to save money that it can seem overwhelming, and once you have saved some money, the process of investing it wisely can be perplexing. The following list will show you some of the all-time best ways to both:

A. Spend money in order to save money.
B. Spend the money you've saved wisely.

1. Have money automatically transferred from your paycheck into a savings account.
2. Contribute to an IRA (even if it's not tax-deductible).
3. Buy a home.
4. Buy and use a home repair manual.
5. Join a credit union.
6. Maintain adequate insurance coverage.
7. Court (and marry) someone who's rich.
8. Buy something *on sale* that you really, truly, absolutely need.
9. Buy used cars.
10. Buy no-load (no-commission) mutual funds.
11. Buy generic and store-brand food, health, beauty, and household products.
12. Buy a newspaper that provides listings of free entertainment.
13. Give your children and grandchildren the best education.
14. Rent (rather than buy) items you use only occasionally.
15. Diversify your investments.
16. Use public transportation.
17. Pay off loans.
18. Invest through a discount broker.
19. Repair rather than replace anything that can be repaired.
20. Maximize your participation in your employer's retirement savings plans.
21. Help your parents out if they're in financial need.
22. Shop around for the best yields on CDs.

23. Pay off your mortgage by the time you retire.
24. Have an attorney prepare your will, durable power of attorney, and living will.
25. Ask to be cremated.

Remember, it's impossible to cut your expenses too much!